PEARLS FROM THE INFINITE WISDOM

Living As Awareness

Volume 2

By

Swami Amritachitswarūpananda Puri

Mata Amritanandamayi Center
San Ramon, California, USA

PEARLS FROM THE INFINITE WISDOM

Living As Awareness

Volume 2

Swami Amritachitswarūpananda Puri

Published by:
Mata Amritanandamayi Center
P.O. Box 613
San Ramon, CA 94583-0613, USA

International: www.amma.org
inform@amritapuri.org

Table of Contents

Foreword

The life of every single person on this planet is an endless series of experiences. For many of us, the challenges of life feel overwhelming, and in seeking solutions, we were somehow fortunate and blessed to land at Amma's holy feet. Unlike many gurus of the past, Amma turns no one away even if their motive in approaching her is to seek solution to their worldly problems. Without us even being aware of it, she works on us to bring us to the spiritual path, guiding us to the Truth that there are no permanent solutions to be found 'out there'. She also does something that is extraordinarily rare, she gives us a glimpse of that divine Love when we are in her arms. We forget ourselves, our problems and are simply dunked in the ocean of divine Love which is Amma.

Inspired by Amma and her disciples, many of us start performing various spiritual practices. We meditate, do japa, perform service to help others and chant. However, the state of love and freedom which we experienced in Amma's arms still seems to be far away from becoming our natural state. Amma repeatedly reminds us that we are the "embodiments of the Self and True Love", yet we somehow are yet to feel that to be the nature of our Being.

When we inquire into why this is so, Amma gives us the answer. Amma says "Just as a seedling can only emerge when the outer shell of the seed breaks open, so too, the Self unfolds when the ego breaks open and disappears." This is a tremendous Truth. It addresses the root of the problem we all face in our spiritual pursuit. The core issue is that if the one who meditates and performs all the spiritual practices is the ego, then the destination is ever far away. The "person" is the problem. The ego is the mind. This is why Amma talks so much about surrender and love.

In this book, Swami Amritachitswarūpanandaji approaches this topic with help from the Gita and the Upanishads. Swamiji has spent decades deeply meditating on the Upanishads and distills their message for the benefit of Amma's children. There are numerous and repeated pointers to the Self. Reading this book is a meditation. I would suggest the same to those who pick up this book. Approach it as a meditation, as an aid to repeatedly remind you of your true nature. The certain amount of repetition is intentional, to help break our deep rooted tendency to think of ourselves as a person.

May this book help many to get in touch with the ever-shining Awareness within, the inner Amma who is Love.

Vikas R, California, USA

Introduction

This book is a continuation of the meditation on Amma's teachings and the timeless Upanishadic wisdom that began in the first volume. The primary topic here is on how to live free, being centered in our True nature. The greatest example of one who lives centered Awareness (SthitaPrajña) is our Divine mother Amma.

In the previous volume, we discussed the nature of the Self, the mind, and the path of Self-enquiry ending with a discussion regarding the role of the Sadguru on the path. In this volume, the focus is on living one's understanding. Although this book continues from the previous one, it is not necessary to read that before starting this book, if one is already familiar with the path of Vedanta. For people new to this path, we highly recommend reading the previous book since we build on some previously introduced concepts.

Through the study, reflection and contemplation on the statement of the scriptures, as the recognition of one's Self-nature dawns within, a person starts to shift their sense of Being. They shift from considering oneself to be of the body-mind, to attempting to live as Awareness. This is the beginning of true freedom. Recognizing one's Self-nature to be of the nature of Being-Awareness-Bliss, and ultimately stabilizing in this understanding is freedom. It is also called the state of Jivanmukti (liberated even while living in the body), of being a SthitaPrajña (established as Awareness) and various other terms in the scriptures. Here, we shall simply look to refer to it as "living as Awareness". This is both the practice and the realization according to the path of non-dual vedanta. With practice, this becomes effortless.

All of us eventually take to the spiritual path because we seek freedom from pain and suffering, and desire happiness and peace. Life often feels to drift without purpose, and pleasure seeking leaves us drained and feeling empty. Many often ask what is the purpose and relevance of studying scriptures written hundreds or thousands of years ago. They are still relevant because the fundamental questions of life have not changed. The problems we all face, irrespective of all the technological advancements over the centuries, have not changed the issues of life.

The following questions are fundamental to all humans, at all times:

Who am I? What is the essential nature of my Being?

What is freedom? How is it attained?

What is my duty, my path in life?

How should I relate to society, the people I live and interact with?

I do various actions, but they do not always go the way I want. Why is this so?

What happens to me when I die?

So the scriptures provide answers to all of these questions and more. Also, not only do they answer these questions, but they answer these questions from different perspectives, in order to assist people of different temperaments and stages of spiritual development.

The Bhagavad Gita is one such scripture. In it, Lord Krishna instructs a spiritually and morally conflicted Arjuna. The study of Bhagavad Gita is an indispensable aid to every spiritual seeker. Amma has encouraged her devotees to study the Gita deeply. Amma says: "The purpose of learning Gita is to become Sri Krishna.". To be Sri Krishna is to know one's essential nature to be the Self, and be free. The 21st verse from the second chapter of the Gita, which is called "Sānkhya Yoga" is a deeply insightful one.

vedāvināśhinaṁ nityaṁ ya enam ajam avyayam
kathaṁ sa puruṣhaḥ pārtha kaṁ ghātayati hanti kam

O Arjuna! He who knows that Atma is birthless, deathless, real, and imperishable, whom can he slay or cause to be slain?

This verse is a direct antidote to Arjuna's despair. Sri Krishna here is addressing the two fundamental misconceptions that are ailing Arjuna. Arjuna does not know the nature of the Self, and Arjuna thinks he is the doer.

Arjuna, due to a lack of Self-knowledge, thinks himself to be a warrior and the son of Pritha (Kunti). He thinks, because he is such a great warrior, he is likely to kill many of his friends and family members, who are now part of the enemy army. So, he wants to avoid the battle. Sri Krishna here tells Arjuna to wake up and see the Truth! "You, O Arjuna, are not a limited individual, and neither are these people who are assembled on the battlefield. Your error here is that you think you are the doer, and as a result of your doing, you will cause certain results. None of these are true."

So then, who is Arjuna? Sri Krishna tells him: "You are the Self! This Self, which is the fundamental essence of all, was never born, nor will it ever die. It is imperishable, indestructible. If you think by the swing of a sword, it can be destroyed, you are solely mistaken. Also, you are not the doer. If you think you are the killer, you are again wrong. You have neither the power to act, nor are you able to cause any desired result from your action." Later on in the third chapter, Sri Krishna again points out that it is due to our misconception, our ignorance, that we think ourselves to be the doer. Nature, Prakriti alone is the doer.

Now, how are we to know that "I" am the Self? The Gita and the Upanishads tell us "Tat Tvam Asi", but we do not get it, we do not recognize our True nature. We are caught up in our identification with the body-mind-world complex, with the concepts of "I" and "mine". This is called superimposition. In simpler words, we are imagining things that are not real.

How do we break free from this? The Mahatmas walk amongst us to show that the words of the scriptures are real, and can be lived. They are not just printed words that were spoken by someone who lived 5200 years ago, but they are verifiable Truths. Mahatmas like Amma are proof that one can live without the body-mind identification and instead live as pure Awareness, pure Love. Infact, Amma begins her every single Satsang with this reminder to us, that we are also the embodiments of pure Love and Self (Prēma Swaroopa and Atma Swaroopa). By studying the lives of such beings and following the instructions of the Guru, one gains the purity of the heart and one-pointedness of mind. With such a clear mind, when one investigates all experiences, discriminating between what's 'Nitya' Eternal and 'anitya' non-eternal, the ever-present Self is revealed. One recognizes this Self to be unborn, indescribable, eternal, immutable. In contrast, the world of names and forms appears, stays for a while, and gets destroyed in time. Even time and space appear in Sat (Truth).

So, this Self-knowledge brought clarity, understanding and enabled Arjuna, the seeker, the conflicted one, to be free and to act as an instrument in the hands of the Lord. Established as the Self, he no longer identified with the roles he needed to play in society, but he still did what had to be done, without the idea of doer-ship, established in equanimity, and accepting whatever results arose from such action. In the same way, when we discard our misconceptions regarding who we are and drop the idea of doer-ship, we find immediate peace and can live life as instruments of the Lord, doing what is appropriate in every situation, free of self-interest.

When discrimination is mentioned, it is usually referred to as the discrimination between the real and the unreal, the Self and the non-Self, ie; atma-anatma-viveka. But what does "unreal" really mean? Is it unreal, like the horns of a rabbit? Or is it a misperception, like a lamppost which is mistaken to be a ghost by a little child in the dark? Advaita Vedanta proclaims that it is indeed a misperception. Mithya, unreal indicates that the world is neither entirely real, like Brahman, nor entirely unreal, like a barren woman's son. It is Anirvacanīya—indescribable. We cannot define this world with absolute certainty; hence, it is logically referred to as Anirvacanīya— indescribable, undefinable. Due to our ignorance, we believe the body-mind-world complex to be real and separate entities. It is as if one sees a wave and believes it to be a real, separate entity. Reality is that the waves are mere expressions of the ocean. Due to the assigning of a name and form to it, one might misperceive the wave to be real and separate.

In the Bhagavad Gita, Sri Krishna says:

īśvaraḥ sarvabhūtānāṃ hṛddeśe'rjuna tiṣṭhati
bhrāmayansarvabhūtāni yantrārūḍhāni māyayā (18:61)

"God dwells in the hearts of all beings, O Arjuna,
causing all beings, by His illusive power, to
revolve, as if mounted on a machine."

This verse is much loved and quoted by the dualistic sects. There is a "God" who dwells in the hearts of all beings, causing everyone to move about and perform actions as if an operator were operating a machine. Then, people are taught to pray to such a God. But if God's nature is truly omnipresence and omniscience, then where is the room for the individual who prays?

And if God is truly the driver of all events, then what is the necessity of prayer? Is not acceptance and surrender the sign of true understanding? So, putting aside the idea of a separate "God" who sits in the bodies of all beings, if one seeks THAT Awareness, the presence that enables this whole phenomenon of the ever-changing body-mind-world complex to occur, then one arrives at the recognition of their own Self nature.

Yet, one may say, I understand what you mean, yet I still perceive all of the beings and things in this world, and I still suffer. If this is the case, one needs to truly look within and ask how deep one's conviction really is. If one is really convinced that their true nature is the Self, which is Awareness, and that all changes perceived are expressions of that ONE awareness, then can there be any objections to what Is?

Some other practitioners look to shut out the perceptions entirely, through the practice of samadhi like states. Again, while there is no objection to the practice of meditation, samadhi and other spiritual practices, what is being pointed out here is that the essence of freedom is the recognition of one's True nature as Awareness. Then, such a being is no longer affected or deluded by the ever-changing body-mind-world complex. True freedom lies in living this understanding.

This is not to say that the study of scriptures and practices such as Japa, meditation, chanting and so on are discouraged. By all means, one should practice these, as they help in the purification and one-pointedness of the mind, which are fundamental to the path. We have covered these prerequisites in the previous volume of the book. Yet, the essence of freedom lies not in this 'doing', but in resting in one's True nature of 'Being'. It is in recognizing one's Self as being ever-pure, ever-free, and abiding as THAT.

How does this ignorance even begin, one may ask? If one is ever-free and ever-pure, how did this ignorance of one's Self nature occur? Sri Sankara says it is in the misidentification of the seer. The seer is the Self, yet it misperceives itself to be a Jiva, and believes the changing body-mind-world complex to be real. In correcting this misperception lies the entirety of the spiritual quest.

Amma always reminds us of our Self-nature and often says "You are not helpless kittens; you are lions! You are not a candle needing to be lit. You are in fact the Self-effulgent sun!". Needless to say, the topics and the discussions here are based on the teachings of Amma and the scriptures.

Much of the content in this book is based on discussions from a satsang group that I often meet to discuss various topics from the scriptures. In some other cases, words would come to me as I reflected on verses from the scriptures or from Amma's satsangs. In such instances, I would often attempt to immediately write down the understanding that dawned within. On occasions, I would scribble something down while I waited in Amma's room. Being in Amma's presence is pure grace, and in her presence, peace and understanding flow without barriers.

The aim of writing this book is to help shift our attitude from considering the body-mind-world complex to be real, to living as Awareness, while looking upon the world as the play of Awareness (Cit-shakti). It is hoped that the present work will be useful to the spiritual seekers in their spiritual quest.

Swami Amritachitswarūpananda Puri,
Amritapuri, Kerala

1. Breaking Free

tyāgenaike amṛtatvamānaśuḥ
By renunciation alone is immortality attained.
– Kaivalya Upanishad

People who walk the spiritual path do so due to the urge to find true fulfillment and to free themselves from the three kinds of suffering - arising from one's body and mind, from society and from nature (Adhyātmika, Adibhautika, Adidaivika). This profound quest for fulfillment requires a supreme effort, for true freedom is the liberation from the mind's projections and the transformation of one's self-perception. Unlike any pursuit in the material world, this journey is an unparalleled endeavor, seeking to transcend the superficial and uncover the eternal truth within.

People who begin the spiritual path often do so like they would pursue anything else in the material world, with a "utility" approach. They seek a great reward at the end of their quest, a great eternal bliss, samādhi, Nirvāna and so on. In such a quest, the ego seeks to find ultimate victory, its greatest accomplishment. As one matures, they realize that freedom and the ego cannot coexist. This Truth is hard to accept, even if one has already performed many spiritual practices.

Amma tells a funny story to illustrate how deep our conditioning often is, despite performing much spiritual practice and scriptural study.

A long time ago, two disciples lived with a realized sage performing spiritual practices, learning the scriptures and serving the sage and his hermitage. One day, the sage sent them both on an errand. When they returned, he found that they were both fiercely quarreling with each other.

When he inquired why? One disciple said 'He hit me!'. The other disciple said 'He called me a monkey!'

The sage shook his head and said 'You both have studied the scriptures with me for over 20 years, and I have taught you hundreds of times that you are not the body or the mind, but the infinite Self itself. Yet, you never believed me. He called you a monkey just once, and you believed him!'

To drop one's dearly held beliefs, concepts and ego- often turns out to be too difficult and too high a price to pay. The popular allegory presented by the Greek philosopher in his book 'Republic' represents this very well.

The Allegory of the Cave by Plato

Plato claimed that awareness gained through the senses is no more than opinion and that, to have real Awareness, one must gain it through a Truth-seeking way of thinking, inquiry, and right-knowledge.

Plato distinguishes between people who mistake the body-mind-world complex perceived by the senses for the Truth, instead of those who seek the Truth behind what is perceived through inquiry and reasoning. In the Brihadaranyaka Upanishad, we see this phrase Satyasya Satyam - 'Truth of the Truth' - Bri Up. 2-4-9, referring to the Truth that is the substratum of all that is perceived, which is the Self (real nature) by discernment.

The cave: In the allegory "The Cave," Plato describes a group of people who have lived chained to the wall of a cave all their lives, facing a blank wall. Their arms and legs are bound, and their heads are tied so that they cannot look at anything but the stonewall in front of them. Since birth, these prisoners have been here and have never been seen outside of the cave. These people watch shadows projected on the wall from objects passing in front of a fire behind them and give names to these shadows. The shadows are the prisoners' reality, but they are not accurate representations of the real world.

The play: Plato suggests that the prisoners would begin a 'play' of guessing which shadow would appear next. If one of the prisoners were to guess correctly, the others would praise him as clever and say that he was a master of nature.

Breaking free: One of the prisoners then escapes from their bindings and leaves the cave. He is shocked at the world he discovers outside the cave and does not believe it can be real. As he becomes used to his new surroundings, he realizes that his former view of reality was wrong.

He begins to understand his new world, sees that the Sun is the source of life, and goes on a journey where he discovers beauty and meaning. He sees that his former life and the guessing play they had is useless.

The return: The prisoner returns to the cave to inform the other prisoners of his findings. They do not believe him and threaten to kill him if he tries to set them free!

Why is this so? Why do people resist the Truth? Resist freedom? Amma says not all are ready. That's why pointing out the Truth needs to be presented in a way that is appealing and in accordance with the level of the listener. Sometimes Truth may be bitter, says Amma. From time immemorial, greater seers and thinkers have been born and shared the Truths they discovered with the people of the world, but accepting them and their ideas has been a great challenge. People are fine with praising, idolizing and even worshiping these great personalities, while at the same time resisting accepting and/or following the Truths shared. Even though the Truth is simple, we miss the logic of seeing reality because of our preconceived notions.

The path of Truth is a solo-journey. We have to be alone to seek the Truth. We need to make some time and create a silent space to reflect and meditate in solitude on the Truths given to us by the wise. Most important of all, we need the willingness to drop our attachments to our ego-centric personalities and opinions.

What keeps us bound?

The body-mind-world complex:

From birth, our personalities are created and crafted by our parents and society, reinforcing the idea of us being the body-mind complex. We bind ourselves to this idea, and normally do not even consider looking beyond it. We are comfortably bound within the familiar. All we do is follow the established routines set by society. School, perhaps college, graduation, a job, marriage, perhaps children, followed by old age, failing health, sickness and a miserable death heavy with the memories of pain and pleasures.

This vicious cycle is the only path that seems to be the option for most. Since birth, rarely do people even get to hear or see the possibility of freedom from these notions and this painful cycle. Freedom, as defined by the world, seems to be the ability to pursue name, fame, wealth, and progeny. While we struggle to attain these, we seek pleasures to keep us fueled, unaware that it is a deception. As Amma says, "it is like buying poison, thinking it to be nectar," because we are unaware of anything beyond, we do not know the silent Awareness within, witnessing it all. Our ignorance is deep-rooted.

Everyone around us moves in this ignorance, and we continue to gather impressions about the body-mind-world complex. Concepts are created about me, not-me, family, money, competition, success, war, and love. Even though everyone is illuminated by the Self-effulgent Awareness, we are unaware of it due to ignorance. We carry out all our activities with the body-mind-world complex, thinking it to be real.

The deception

We get deluded because we cannot perceive anything beyond our sensory inputs. When a dog sees its reflection in a mirror, it barks at it believing it to be real. In a similar manner, we see the world in front of us, and thus we take it to be real. Our reality is only confined to whatever feedback we receive about ourselves from others. Thus, we remain victims of the fingers pointed at us by others. Believing in the delusion of concepts held by society and holding strong to the erroneous belief that the world exists to cater to our demands, we are completely lost.

The net result of such living is that we are constantly in fear and ego-centric most of the time. This is reflected in the world we see around us, filled with many wars and unhappiness.

We work seriously, believing in the idea of a real world out there that can provide happiness and fulfillment, accepting each other's ignorance, and expecting people to reward us when we acknowledge the world of names and forms. Every interaction is colored with the question, "What's in it for me?". Attention from the opposite gender, desire to be appreciated, to dominate others, suppress those who disagree with our aims or beliefs—this game continues endlessly, seeking for gain. Some we encounter may accept and reward us; others denounce us and take away what we have. These power struggles and wars have ruined humans, but we are still not ready to give them up.

Breaking free

It is a brave being who reflects on all these flaws of society, separates oneself from others, creates space for oneself and starts thinking,

So, Katha Upanishad 2-1-1 says:

parāñci khāni vyatṛṇatsvayambhū stasmāt
parāṅ paśyati nāntarātman |
kaściddhīraḥ pratyagātmānama ikṣad
āvṛtta cakśur amṛtatvamicchan ||

The self-existent one (Ishwara, the God) created our
senses to look outward, which is why we see the world
around us and not the Atman (inner Self) within. A
wise person, wanting to achieve immortality, turns
their attention inward and sees the Atman within.

In other words, while our senses naturally make us look outside,
some discerning individuals manage to look within and find
their true inner Self, pratyagatman. According to the Sruti,
which declares the derivative meaning of the term "atman," it is
specifically used to refer to this inner Self, not anything else. The
Atman is what pervades everything and ensures the continuous
existence of the universe. This is why it is called the Atman.

The aspirant inquires,

What is this vicious cycle of stupidity where we all end up
unhappy?

Who am I? What is the essential nature of my Being?

What is freedom? How is it attained?

What is my duty, my path in life?

How should I relate to society, the people I live and interact
with?

I do various actions, but they do not always go the way I
want. Why is this so?

What happens to me when I die?

Seeking answers and inner peace, such a being seeks out a
Guru to learn from. It is mentioned in the Sruti that only one
who has a teacher will know the truth (ācāryavānpuruṣo veda
Ch Up 6.14.2). Life mysteriously seems to assist such a seeker and

arranges contact with a true Guru to show the genuine seeker the way to freedom.

When one starts traversing the path of Truth, it is initially difficult because the long reinforced habits of taking the body-mind-world complex to be real act as obstacles on the path. Slowly the Guru disciplines the seeker and shows how to relax and purify the mind through selfless service and meditation.

To be eligible for perceiving the Truth, one needs mind and sense control, forbearance, faith in the words of scriptures and teachers, patience, tranquility, discernment, dispassion towards the world, and passion for knowing the Truth as Self-nature. We have covered these topics extensively in volume 1.

Then one begins understanding nature of Self and finds freedom from suffering.

Free from craving and desire

The state of Jivanmukti (liberated while still living in the body) is not imagined or visualized, nor is it something assigned to one through tradition, public opinion, or a matter of personal belief. One cannot say, 'I am convinced I am liberated, I have met all the parameters of liberation. I have performed seva, much Japa, Tapas, meditation, and experienced XYZ states of mind; thus, I am relaxed, I have no more struggles, and I am liberated.' This is not how the state of Jivanmukti works!

The nature of the Self is ever free by nature. While the nature of the body-mind-world complex is ever changing, in a state of constant flux. The nature of the Self on the other hand, is never subject to modifications or change. This is why the Self is not a state to be attained, but instead, it is to be known and understood. It is not something that is granted by anyone, nor is it a title conferred by somebody. Nor is it something that descends down onto us through prayer. The recognition of Self-nature simply occurs simultaneously with hearing the Sruti (the Upanishads) and gaining scriptural wisdom from a teacher or Guru, who reveals the identicalness of one's real nature with Brahman, the absolute reality, as expressed in the statement 'Tat Tvam Asi.' This recognition negates ignorance and leads to the understanding of one's own true nature through right knowledge.

Once again, it is important to reiterate that prayers, participating in seva activities, Japa, etc. are all helpful. They bring about purification and one-pointedness of mind, which create the groundwork for helping one recognize their True Self-nature. All I want to emphasize here is that the means should not become the goal.

What is the right way, then, to understand this state of freedom? There is a beautiful Sanskrit phrase called 'Na Dveshti Na kankshati' in the Bhagavad Gita 5:3. This means one neither has an aversion nor a desire for any object of experience. When one understands one's Self-nature to be the ever pure Awareness and not the individualized ego, then such a being, even though living in the body and interacting with the body-mind-world complex, does not look to it with either craving or aversion. Instead, the thoughts, sensations, emotions and feelings that arise from one's own-body mind as well as society around him or her are simply perceived and allowed to pass.

So this contemplation of 'Na Dveshti Na kankshati' - 'No aversion, nor desire'—is important. Whatever the spiritual practices one follows, one's choices should not be driven by one's preferences or by one's likes and dislikes. Here, the refutation or denial of the untruth is based on the viewpoint of Self-nature. The standpoint of the Self is only the criterion, instead of trying to uphold any particular theory or deny another. We are not advocating any particular theory of preference here. We are discussing the right knowledge by knowing which we will know the Self-nature in its entirety. By knowing Self-nature, we will know everything. If we realize the nature of Self, we recognize everything, 'sarvam' because Self is the Self of all. So the focus here is on this completeness, this 'arivu' or 'knowingness' by itself, is intrinsically complete. This understanding should become firm in its entirety.

The Chandogya Upanishad (3.14.1) declares 'Sarvam Khalvidam Brahma'. That is, there is no such thing as an 'object' in this world. Instead, everything (Sarvam) is in essence the nature of the Self, of the THE TRUE NATURE OF BRAHMAN. In essence, everything is 'thou' in 'Thou art that'!

The search for Freedom

Most people love the idea of freedom and want to be free, but their understanding along with the commonly held beliefs regarding freedom are based on false ideas. We build up concepts based on false ideas, then seek validation and certification from others, hoping they affirm our wrong concepts. In the name of education, rewards and status, we get totally carried away by the false. We mutually reinforce each other's ignorance and live in a false world. Whatever aspect of life one considers, be it global, economics, politics or education, all we seem to be engaged in is a mutual validation of each other's false concepts and ignorance.

It is like the blind leading the blind. Is this not obvious when one truly investigates them? This also carries over onto the spiritual field. People want to know precisely what "Truth" is. They look for definitions of Truth to be handed to them, believing Truth to be yet another concept they can consume, just like every other concept that they have consumed during their lives. Even though the truth is indescribable, the Upanishads attempt to point to the Truth through statements that act as key pointers. Some examples:

Prajñānam Brahma - Awareness is Brahman;
Aham Brahmasmi - I am Brahman (Supreme Self);
Ayam Atmā Brahma - this Self (Atma) is Brahman;

Brahma Satyam Jagan Mithyā - Brahman is real; the world is illusory;
Brahma Satyam Jagat Satyam - Brahman is Real; the world is also real from the standpoint of the Self.
ekam evadvitīyam Brahma - Brahman is one, without a second.
Soham - He is I
sarvam khalvidam Brahma - All of this is Brahman.
na jāyathe - The Self is never born nor dies.
nasato vidyate bhāvo nabhāvo vidyate satah - The unreal, although appearing to exist, has in reality no existence. The real, though not an object to senses, never ceases to exist. The perfect knowledge of both is seen by the knowers of Truth.
Atma Ithi eva upāsita - Meditate on your Self as the supreme Truth

People seem to prefer being spoon fed concepts instead of using such pointers to dive deep within themselves and probe the Truth regarding their own true Self, and the illusory, ever-changing body-mind-world complex. Why is this so? Why is it that people would rather consume concepts fed to them and imagine Truth through ideas, images, persons and places? Through all such concepts, all one succeeds in doing is distancing oneself from the Truth. Is this not a wonder? One starts by seeking to know the Truth, but due to only being familiar with the normal way concepts are consumed in the world, all one succeeds in doing is going farther away from finding freedom and relief from suffering. It is like walking south while seeking to go to the Himalayas! [This statement assumes one is in South India; the Himalayas are to the north.]

Sri Sankara describes this in his commentary on the Taittiriya Upanishad

mṛgatṛṣṇāmbhasi snātaḥ kha-puṣpa-kṛta-śekharaḥ |
eṣa vandhyā-suto yāti śaśa-śṛṅga-dhanurdharaḥ ||

There goes this barren woman's son, who has bathed in
mirage waters, wears a laurel made from sky flowers,
and holds a bow fashioned from a rabbit horn.
- Taittiriya Bhashyam, Sankara-2.1.1

So it appears that both our worldly and spiritual pursuits are
based on false notions. We are seeking freedom while holding
on strongly to concepts that strengthen the reality of the body-
mind-world complex. But freedom is the Truth that we are never
the body-mind-world complex and are of the nature of being
ever free. Due to our tight grip on false beliefs, all our efforts to
reach the Truth become futile.

However, due to the nature of the subtlety of Truth, most
people find it difficult. This is because anything that one can
think or do to "arrive" at the Truth moves one away from the
Truth. There is no "doing" in Truth, only Being. It is so obvious
in nature, as it is the first, foremost, and most direct. So to know
it, there is no other way than through discernment.

There is no other way, because all the other ways which
involve 'doing' veils the Truth. We have to see very clearly.

Why is this so? This is because in order for any "doing,"
there also needs to be a "doer," which is the ego, the "I," the
Jiva, believing in the reality of itself and the world around it.
We have to negate this whole falsehood. Otherwise, all of these
beliefs and concepts about ourselves, the world around us, and
the world from which one "attains" freedom are false. All this
become obstacles to the direct recognition of the Truth. This is
why the truth is described as "satyasya satyam" (Bṛhadāraṇyaka
Upaniṣad 2-1-20) the truth of the Truth, the essence.

Therefore, if we claim that all our actions, words, beliefs, and
so forth are motivated by a pursuit of truth, this claim is false, as
none of these actions bring us any closer to the truth. If we cling
to such beliefs, we block our freedom with our own attitudes and
actions. All such actions are akin to fighting against the wind or

space. Each blow we try to land only helps to leave us fatigued and does nothing to affect the wind or space. Similarly, when we express complaints such as "I am depressed or anxious," "something has not come my way," or "it is not yet my time, the right time has to come," these are all delusions rooted in false concepts we have constructed about ourselves and the world.

So it is important to reflect on these fundamental questions: Is there such a thing as the Truth? Does this Truth depend on time, place, or person? Does the Truth depend on any of my concepts? What holds us back from recognizing the Truth?

Due to our erroneous notions, we think certain things—certain relationships, some places, or certain incidents that happened in the past—hold us back from realizing the Truth. Can the Truth really be blocked by these things? Is there any such thing that can hold back the Truth? Or are there any such things that, if we were to only complete them, like certain commitments or acquire certain new advanced yoga techniques, or if we were to only be in a certain holy place or whatever, we would be able to realize the Truth. Can this ever be true? Or we project things onto the Guru and so on, and claim someone can give us the Truth, give us freedom.

The Upanishads inform, 'Tat Twam Asi' - You are that ever-free reality, in reality. Can we really hold onto beliefs, concepts, stories, fairy tales or fantasies and realize this ever-present Truth?

Apart from the false belief that we "attain" Self-realization through certain kinds of actions, by doing spiritual practices, charity, seva, etc., there is another often held belief, and this is regarding devotion and surrender. Can we really say 'I shall surrender, and then freedom will come? Truth will descend upon us because we have surrendered. Now the Guru should take responsibility for me because I have totally surrendered.' Can it happen that way? Is surrender another "doing" that one does, which then will result in freedom? Is there any Truth in these things? It is important to clearly see that all these things are false. If we really see the false as false, we are free. That is real freedom.

Keeping these false beliefs, achievements, and ideas, how can one be free? We sought out the spiritual path because of the beatings and suffering experienced from a materialistic way of living. We approach the spiritual path with similar concepts of "doing" and "achieving." But the Self we wanted to find is imperceptible, for It is never perceived; undecaying, for It never decays; unattached, for It is never attached; unfettered—it never feels pain and never suffers injury. So, by 'Neti, Neti' (Bṛhadāraṇyaka Upanishad 4.5.15) approach, 'Not this, not this', we need to free ourselves from false ideas and concepts.

Freedom is right here now. Wherever Truth is, freedom also is. When we clearly see through these delusions and rest with what Is, we rest as That Truth. That is total freedom, which is freedom from the false. Freedom from the unreal. Freedom from ignorance. Freedom from concepts.

An Investigation into Suffering

The Buddha, Siddhartha Gautama, when he investigated the reality of one's daily living, realized that suffering was inseparable from the experience of samsara. When we look into our own lives, we also see that this is so. Despite our best efforts to accumulate pleasant objects, people and experiences around us, we find that it is very difficult to sustain a state of pleasure, and that it inevitably brings with it pain and suffering.

The Buddha said, desire was the cause of suffering. In other circumstances, he also stated that ignorance was the cause of suffering. Vedanta states the same Truth.

Question: What is this ignorance? Why does it create suffering?

Answer: Suffering is due to the incorrect identification of one's Self with the body-mind-world complex. That is, when we forget our Self-nature and identify with the non-self, believing ourselves to be individuals, we suffer. We then try to cling to this individuality, seeking happiness from accumulating pleasant objects, people, and experiences while striving to avoid unpleasant objects, people, and experiences. Anytime we fail in our efforts to hold onto the pleasant and avoid the unpleasant, we suffer. So we suffer when changes in our bodies, minds, and the world are contrary to our expectations.

We are unaware or we forget, that change is the very nature of the body-mind-world complex. We invest so much into all this that we suffer every time things change according to their nature. We thought we were them and that they belonged to us. We categorize everything into 'me' and 'not-me,' 'mine' and 'not-mine.'

Question: How can we escape from this suffering?

Answer: Suffering is avoided by having the awareness that suffering is primarily related to the ego (identification with the body-mind complex), which is also transient. There is no suffering in You (Self), says the Guru and the Upanishads. Suffering has no reality itself. We give it reality, and it becomes real. That is, we superimpose our reality on suffering. Once we assume this suffering to be real, it strengthens depending on our attention we give. Our attention being our continued brooding on the believed cause of suffering. If we stop giving it reality, suffering ceases, akin to ceasing to chase after mirages once we understand them to be mere appearances, without any real water.

Question: What do you mean by suffering having no reality? Can you definitively respond to the question whether suffering really exists or not?

Answer: Pain exists. Suffering does not. Pain is experienced. Suffering is imagined. So, Krishna says to Arjuna in the Gita:

aśhochyān-anvaśhochas-tvaṁ prajñā-vādānśh cha bhāṣhase
gatāsūn-agatāsūnśh-cha nānuśhochanti paṇḍitāḥ
–Bhagavad Gita: 2, Verse 11

You grieve for those who should not be grieved
for, yet you speak words of wisdom. The wise
lament neither for the living nor for the dead.

Arjuna is grieving for those who do not deserve grief, indicating his misunderstanding of the nature of the Self. Krishna points out that although Arjuna speaks wise words, he is not truly wise because the truly wise do not lament for the living or the dead. The wise, having the knowledge of the Self (Atman), understand that the Self is eternal and unchanging, hence there is no reason for sorrow.

"Ashochyan" refers to those who are not worthy of sorrow because they are either eternal (the Atman) or temporal (the body), which undergoes natural cycles of birth and death. The "Panditah" or the wise ones, who perceive the true nature of reality, do not lament because they see beyond the dualities of life and death.

In essence, there is a need for the knowledge of the eternal Self, which transcends physical existence and thereby eliminates sorrow.

By imparting the true wisdom of the eternal Self, Arjuna's misconception is removed. This wisdom, taught by the Guru, reveals the eternal truth necessary for transcending suffering. Understanding and realizing the nature of the Self as eternal, unchanging, and beyond physical existence can lead to the end of all sorrow and suffering.

It is only the Guru, with their profound understanding and insight, who can impart this eternal truth and guide us towards ending suffering. The Guru's teachings illuminate the path to Self-realization, making it possible to transcend the ephemeral and connect with the eternal essence of our being. Thus, ultimate liberation and peace are attained through the knowledge of the Self, as bestowed by the Guru.

Question: What is the Truth?

Truth is That which is unchanging. That which changes is not our nature, and we witness that change.

Question: How?

All thoughts, emotions, feelings and sensations are known.

Question: So what?

Answer: If they are known, we are not them.

Question: How?

Answer: Say there is a book in front of me. I know the book, so I am not the book. This is obvious to everyone. It is an object being perceived. Similarly, the mind and its activity are perceived by 'me.' So I am not them.

Question: Is it not part of our nature?

No, it is not our true nature. The body-mind-world complex has its own nature, which is one of constant change. They are always in a state of flux.

Question: But I want a solution to this problem of suffering. Is there a solution?

Answer: Yes, the solution is to know that 'I am free of these thoughts, emotions and feelings.' Be free from this idea of being a separate self.

Question: What do you mean?

Answer: Recognize that the problems you have during the waking state are non-existent in the dream state. Similarly, during deep sleep, the problems of neither the waking state nor the dream state affect me, yet I exist as 'I am.'

Question: This is no answer! These troubles still exist for me when I wake up?

Answer: Then do what is necessary to dispel them, if possible. But recognize that this is not always possible. To think that the body-mind-world can change to suit one's desires is suffering.

Question: But I am seeking a way to overcome my problems and dispel this suffering?

Answer: Who told you that you would overcome all the problems and subsequently experience peace?

Question: What do you mean?

Answer: They come and go. Their nature is so. They arise and cease, according to their nature. We think we have to overcome them, which causes delusional ideas that we have to do something. We have to understand that the nature of each thing is unique and cannot be changed. Learning this way is called discernment. Through discernment, we come out of the problem.

In Self, there is no problem. So the perspective with which we look at all experiences is important.

It is essential to understand that the mere experience of problems is not the 'gold standard' to claim that they exist or to establish their existence.

Question: Why not? I experience these problems; hence, they exist.

Answer: Nightmares and mirages are experienced, this does not mean that they have reality.

Question: Yet fear was palpable; why?

Answer: The reason is ignorance that there is something out there that has a separate, independent existence.

Question: How does one overcome this fear?

Answer: See the Truth that they don't have a separate, independent existence; they only appear like a picture on the screen.

Listen deeply to the Truths expounded by the Guru and the Upanishads, which point to the Self as the Self of all. Through doing so, one begins to appreciate the Truth. This shifts one's understanding from the body-mind-world complex to the Self as being one's essential nature.

The recognition that our identification with the body-mind-world complex is the root cause of suffering is the way out of ignorance. There is no suffering when one rests as the Self. Despite the continued appearance and disappearance of pain and pleasure, the 'Self' is ever-present, ever pure, ever

Consciousness, ever free of appearances. This conviction regarding reality is freedom.

2. The Self is all there is

From the vantage point of Truth, distinctions like time and space, hierarchy, or the separation between "I" and "You" dissolve into insignificance. These are mere illusions, super-imposed upon the underlying reality. Through the path of negation, known as Neti-Neti, we unravel the essence of Truth (Satsaya Satyam) free from illusion.

Within the realm of completeness, all acts of hearing and listening unfold seamlessly. Even Maya, the illusion itself, is encompassed within this wholeness, devoid of a separate existence. However, in the grand scheme of things, Maya is inconsequential, for it holds no sway over the ultimate reality.

This comprehension is crucial for our spiritual journey, allowing us to transcend the veils of illusion and grasp the fundamental truth that underpins all existence.

Death only touches those who perceive themselves as bound by limitations. However, for those who realize their identity as Brahman, Death holds no power. In the realm of Brahman, duality ceases to exist; there are no beginnings or endings, no conflicts or wars. Brahman encompasses all; there is no "otherness" within it.

Every action we undertake, whether mundane tasks like eating or profound spiritual practices like meditation, occurs within the sphere of Brahman. There is no existence outside of this ultimate reality. Thus, one does not attain completeness; rather, one realizes their inherent completeness. It is the eternal presence of awareness that constitutes the ultimate reality.

Why do we engage in the acts of hearing and listening? Some may question, especially if everything is already complete. However, it's crucial to recognize that all transactions, including the act of listening, stem from the inherent completeness of existence. When we lack awareness of this fundamental truth, we perceive these activities as occurring independently, in fragmented and separate ways.

The absence of awareness regarding the completeness of existence leads us to mistakenly believe that we are limited and incomplete. We feel compelled to fulfill these perceived deficiencies, unaware that our true nature is already whole and complete.

From the moment we awaken with the effulgence of "I" in waking until we drift into slumber, a myriad of experiences unfold—sounds, sensations, sights, tastes, and scents—all weaving together with life. But does the presence of completeness imply that these diverse experiences should cease to exist? Not at all; that's not the message here.

Completeness does not necessitate the absence of variety. Rather, it embraces all possibilities within its expansive embrace. Despite the ceaseless ebb and flow of experiences, completeness remains unwavering. It is ever-complete, untouched by the fluctuations of the world.

Even amidst the turmoil of wars and conflicts, the essence of completeness remains unchanged. Simply acknowledging the reality of Brahman does not magically eradicate these worldly challenges. Wars, along with our everyday struggles, persist as part of life's intricate shades.

However, understanding the principle of completeness does shift our perspective. We no longer perceive these challenges as signs of incompleteness or deficiency. Instead, we recognize them as integral aspects of existence, each playing its role in the grand scheme of things.

Acknowledging Brahman does not exempt us from engaging with the world. We still navigate life's complexities, adhering to the principles of justice and law. Like players in a game or characters in a story, we follow the rules that govern our interactions, ensuring peace and harmony for all.

In this framework, justice and constitutional morality guide our actions. We uphold principles of fairness, ensuring that both reward and punishment are meted out according to rightful measures. Thus, while Brahman remains the eternal reality, our engagement with the world reflects a commitment to ethical conduct and societal harmony.

We're not suggesting that there's incompleteness now so that I can eventually become Brahman. Nor do we propose that, upon becoming Brahman, everything miraculously becomes complete, leading to enlightenment. Therefore, this knowledge serves simply to unveil reality clearly. We're not implying that one will transform into a new Brahman. This notion of becoming complete in that sense is not what Sruti, Upanishads say here.

We're not elevating the individual, with its myriad notions and experiences of joy and sorrow within the body-mind-world complex, to the status of Brahman or God. We're not transforming them into something else entirely. Rather, what we're doing is dismantling the false perceptions and ignorance they hold about themselves. Despite the illusion of being a separate self, the truth is that they are Brahman. Our aim is to negate this illusion of individuality, revealing the inherent oneness with Brahman.

In our spiritual journeys, we often fall into the trap of perceiving everything as separate and distinct, dividing our lives into compartments where empirical activities are seen as different from spiritual ones. This fragmented view leads us to treat practices such as meditation, prayer, chanting, worship and devotional singing as isolated spiritual activities. We mistakenly believe that these practices exist independently of one another, failing to see the unity that underlies them all. However, if we continue to view these practices as separate entities, we cannot hope to experience the oneness they are meant to reveal.

We tend to compartmentalize our spiritual experiences: morning rituals are seen as separate from chanting, seva as distinct from spiritual practices, and devotional singing is considered unrelated to meditation. We delineate between different aspects of our spiritual journey, such as bhajans, white flower meditation, satsangs, ashram life, and worldly life, considering them all separate. This fragmented way of thinking, however, is an illusion that needs to be dissolved. The essence of spiritual practice lies in recognizing the unity that transcends these apparent differences.

When we visit a temple, like the Kali temple, we often perceive Kali as separate from ourselves, and ourselves as separate from others. We create divisions between ourselves and Mahatmas like Amma, and between different aspects of our lives, such as satsang and daily life. But by maintaining these divisions, we obstruct the realization of oneness. The question then arises: where will the realization of unity come from if we continue to uphold these distinctions? The ancient teaching "Tat Tvam Asi" (You are That) emphasizes this inherent unity, revealing that the distinctions we perceive are merely illusions.

When we view the body-mind-world complex, the God, and the scriptures as separate entities, and perceive various spiritual practices as distinct, we inadvertently create conflict within ourselves. We fall into the trap of pitting one against the other, struggling to reconcile these perceived differences. This fragmented perception prevents us from experiencing the inherent unity of all aspects of our existence. In essence, the very things we say are different cannot be made one if we continue to see them as separate.

Our perceptions are often skewed, leading to a divergence between how we see things and how we interpret them. This divergence creates a fragmented existence, where we live amidst divisions and continue along our paths without ever realizing the unity that exists beneath the surface. We assert that these divisions are merely illusions, emphasizing that in reality, such divisions do not exist. Otherwise, even our understanding of Brahman becomes distorted, moving us from one illusion to another, from one darkness to another, as we segregate everything into distinct entities.

When we perceive the God as separate from ourselves while categorizing our empirical life activities into a different realm, we reinforce the reality of birth and death, happiness and sorrow. We become entangled in conflicts, confusion, and afflictions, as if they are inseparable parts of our existence. These struggles cling to us because we have created them, perpetuating the illusion of separateness and division.

By fragmenting our perception of reality, we distance ourselves from Brahman, the ultimate reality. This separation allows desire and aversion, likes and dislikes, anger and attachment to take root within us. We have given these emotions undue reality, nurturing them with the nutrients of separation and division. We see God and ourselves as distinct, leading us to question: where then is Brahman? We search frantically, as if with a microscope, unable to discern it with our naked eyes. Yet, Brahman exists as the grandest truth, overshadowing all else in its vastness and magnificence.

The key to spiritual realization lies in dissolving these illusions of separation and embracing the unity that underlies all aspects of our existence. By recognizing that everything—our thoughts, practices, relationships, and experiences—are expressions of the same infinite reality, we can transcend the limitations of our fragmented perception and experience the oneness that is the essence of Brahman. This realization is not just an intellectual understanding but a lived experience, where we see the divine in everything and everything in the divine, leading us to a state of true spiritual awakening.

Just as we cannot truly confine the infinite expanse of space within the boundaries of a single room, even if we fill that room with countless objects and then claim there's no space left, we often mistakenly believe that space is limited. Despite the immeasurable vastness of the cosmos, filled with galaxies, stars, and planets, our perception becomes confined to the limits of that one room. We declare that space is full, with no room to spare.

Similarly, Brahman, the ultimate reality, embodies completeness and infinite existence. Yet, in our limited understanding, we attempt to carve out spaces within this infinite reality for the place we dwell, ourselves, and various spiritual practices such as Japa (chanting) and Tapa (austerities). We reserve mental space for our preferences, our attachments, our struggles, and even the conflicts we engage in, believing these to be separate and distinct.

However, just as the perception of limited space in the room is an illusion, so too is the idea that we can compartmentalize Brahman. The true understanding lies in recognizing that all these distinctions—our likes and dislikes, our spiritual practices, and even our sense of self—are mere constructs within the infinite expanse of Brahman. To truly comprehend reality, we must negate these notions, dispel the illusions that confine us, and embrace the boundless, undivided nature of existence as it truly is.

We're constantly negating incompleteness, recognizing that within completeness, there's no room for anything less. That's why completeness remains steadfast, whether in the vast expanse of nature with its trees, plants, animals, birds, and humans, or in any other aspect of existence. Never has completeness been tarnished or tainted by incompleteness. It remains whole and untouched.

We must deeply reflect on this truth and diligently work to dispel all illusions. Only by shedding these illusions can we create space for Brahman to reside within us. However, if we persist in clinging to illusions, there'll be no room for Brahman to dwell, for we've filled that sacred space with falsehoods. So, let us clear away the illusions, making way for the eternal presence of Brahman within us.

We've constructed everything in our minds—the concept of God, the intricacies of the body-mind-world complex. We've woven a phenomenon of imagination, filling our lives with these constructs and attributing meaning to every activity. It's imperative that we pause and reflect on these notions, gaining a deeper understanding of our actions and intentions.

We assert that all these activities unfold within the realm of completeness. They're manifestations of the totality of existence. Therefore, we must perceive them from the vantage point of that absolute reality, not from the limited perspective of our constructed realities. It's akin to viewing the world from the standpoint of the Sun, where time is irrelevant and imperfections cease to exist.

Instead, when we observe the Sun from our human perspective, we perceive the cycle of morning, afternoon, and night, attributing transitions and limitations to its brilliance. However, in the Sun's inherent completeness, such fluctuations are non-existent. We impose these fluctuations upon the Sun, failing to recognize its eternal radiance. Similarly, in the presence of the Absolute reality, all activities unfold seamlessly, devoid of limitations and imperfections.

In the realm of completeness, where perfection reigns supreme, there is no room for shortcomings to exist. So, where do these perceived flaws originate? They stem from our own creation, born out of the illusion of separateness that we have woven into our lives. As long as this illusion persists, true completeness remains elusive. Thus, it becomes imperative to dispel this illusion, to remove the veil that shrouds our vision of reality.

This illusion is akin to an eclipse, obscuring the brilliance of the Sun momentarily and casting darkness upon the world. However, in truth, nothing can diminish the radiant glow of the Sun. Similarly, when we close our eyelids, darkness envelops us, albeit temporarily. These illusions are inconsequential from the Sun's perspective, just as they are negligible when we close our eyes.

Yet, for us, these illusions hold sway over our perceptions. We perceive ourselves as separate entities, distinct from the God, the scriptures, and others. This illusion drives us to engage in various practices and rituals, seeking solace and enlightenment. Until we cast aside these illusions, Brahman remains obscured, existing only as a faint mirage amidst the vast desert of our misconceptions.

We may believe that we are engaging in practices aimed at attaining Brahman, but in reality, we are ensnared by the veil of illusion. Even in our pursuit of Brahman, we project our illusions onto the path, clouding our understanding. This veil of ignorance, known as Maya, shrouds our perception, preventing us from realizing the truth.

To dispel this illusion, we must truly grasp the essence of our teachings. We must strip away all limitations and divisions that we impose upon ourselves. Whether it's the distinctions between God and oneself or the artificial divides of state, country, sect, and religion, humanity seems driven to carve out separate identities. We cling to these identities like badges of honour, enhancing our differences through superficial markers.

Is Brahman ensnared in the same illusions that afflict us? Certainly not. Brahman is untouched by deception, for it embodies completeness in its purest form. Our illusions, on the other hand, lead us to erroneously proclaim, "I am ignorant," or to attach labels to ourselves and others. However, the essence of life is absolute completeness, and it's from this vantage point that we must perceive.

Whether it's the majestic trees, delicate flowers, diverse animals, or myriad gods, all emanate from the same source of oneness and completeness. The observer and the observed are both manifestations of this inherent completeness. It's not in their external forms but in their fundamental nature that they embody completeness. Just as all waves are inherently composed of water, so too is everything infused with completeness.

However, if we continue to dwell in illusions, we remain trapped in the cycle of birth and death, plagued by endless problems. That's why it's crucial to recognize and dispel these illusions. We cannot accurately describe the state of being when we transcend limitations and bask in the radiance of completeness. It transcends verbal expression, for it is beyond words.

In essence, completeness and wholeness are synonymous with Brahman—eternal, boundless, and imbued with being, knowing, and bliss. Embracing this truth dispels illusions and liberates us from the cycle of suffering. With unwavering conviction, we declare, "In me, such illusions do not exist, for I am the infinite nature of Brahman. Being-knowing-bliss is my essence, and in this realization, there is no room for illusion."

How can one boldly declare, "I am Brahman, the epitome of completeness, free from illusion," when God is revered as the highest being? This assertion stems from the profound understanding that in the realm of completeness—Brahman—all distinctions dissolve. In this enlightened state of awareness, where the knowledge of completeness reigns supreme, reverence towards a higher being or God transcends illusion.

In this realization, there is no room for doubt or hesitation. It is the courage born of profound understanding—the courage to acknowledge one's true nature as Brahman and to honour the completeness that resides within oneself, others, and God alike.

In this realm, there is no concept of more or less, for completeness knows only abundance and the infinite. Every expression, every interaction, and every moment is suffused with the infinite richness of completeness.

Hence, with unwavering courage, one engages in prayers to the God. How is this possible? It is not through a fragmented mindset but rather with a unified perspective. Just as one's nature is completeness, there is no differentiation of any kind.

Therefore, free from all illusions, every activity unfolds effortlessly. Whether it is giving and receiving, coming and going, eating and drinking, or waking and sleeping, all occur seamlessly within the expansive embrace of completeness.

Therefore, the act of receiving blessings from the Guru or God and bestowing blessings upon others occurs within the realm of one completeness, Brahman. Understanding this truth does not diminish our respect and reverence; rather, it amplifies it.

Hence, we remain grounded in empirical activities, recognizing that empirical behavior unfolds within its own domain. There is no need for egoistic assertions or hierarchical distinctions in the boundless expanse of completeness.

Consider a small pot containing 100 ml of water and a larger pot holding one liter. Despite their varying capacities, both pots are made of the same substance—mud. Similarly, regardless of the differences in their empirical nature, they both serve their purpose according to their respective capacities. The small pot performs actions on a smaller scale, while the larger pot accommodates larger actions.

There is no sense of competition or comparison between them; each operates according to its inherent characteristics. Similarly, animals act in accordance with their animal nature, humans in accordance with human nature, flowers as flowers, and trees as trees. Yet, amidst this diversity, there is no illusion.

Observing the beauty and harmony of nature, we recognize its selfless abundance. As humans endowed with the capacity for perception, we have the privilege of experiencing the completeness that permeates everything around us.

In reality, there is no hierarchy of superiority or inferiority. The notion of one being higher and another lower is a construct of the human mind, devoid of any inherent truth. While it may serve practical purposes in certain contexts, it should never be wielded as a tool for discrimination or prejudice.

It's essential for us, as humans, to recognize the artificiality of these divisions and remain mindful of their transactional nature. They exist merely for the facilitation of societal functioning and should never be used to sow seeds of hatred or animosity. True awareness entails transcending the realm of likes and dislikes, refusing to harbour biases towards any being or entity.

Any mindset that breeds a sense of superiority over others or denigrates certain beings as deficient is inherently flawed. It perpetuates the illusion of separateness and feeds into the cycle of ignorance. True enlightenment lies in acknowledging the interconnectedness of all existence and embracing the inherent completeness present in every being.

Therefore, it is incumbent upon us to cultivate an awareness that transcends these illusions. By aligning ourselves with the Truth, we free ourselves from the shackles of ignorance and discrimination, paving the way for genuine harmony and unity.

Mutual respect and understanding among individuals are paramount, allowing for the seamless execution of all empirical actions. However, it's essential to recognize that within the completeness of Brahman, there are no shortcomings or disparities such as high-low or gain-loss.

Any notions of superiority or inferiority based on societal roles or spiritual status are mere constructs of the human mind and hold no sway in the realm of ultimate reality. There is no inherent superiority, nor is there any inherent inferiority in being a human or holding any other role in society.

To truly grasp the essence of Brahman completeness, one must transcend these illusions of hierarchy and recognize the inherent divinity and completeness present in all beings, irrespective of their outward roles or statuses. It is through this lens of equality and unity that true harmony and fulfillment can be achieved.

Will the authority and reverence of the God diminish if we view it through the lens of completeness? Absolutely not. The nature of the God remains steadfast, unaffected by any perceived fluctuations in status or hierarchy.

When we analyze from the perspective of completeness, the illusion of human superiority or inferiority dissipates. There is no inherent hierarchy where God is superior and I am inferior; such distinctions fade away in the face of wholeness.

In this understanding, both oneself and the God are embodiments of wholeness. Therefore, there is no concept of more or less within this realm of completeness.

When mutual respect and acknowledgment of completeness prevail, the notion of high and low, superior and inferior, loses its relevance, paving the way for harmony and unity among all beings.

The God remains untouched by such illusions. Whether people prostrate before him, chant thousands of names, or criticize, God ever remains devoid of any illusion.

By embracing the truth of completeness, we negate these illusions. We must realize and affirm within ourselves that we do not harbor such fantasies. Whether we evaluate ourselves as superior or inferior, it is all part of the illusion that must be dispelled.

This conviction should be deeply ingrained within us. Only then can we transcend the illusion of self-importance and recognize the inherent divinity within ourselves and others.

We often fall into the trap of comparing ourselves to others, measuring our worth based on superficial factors such as political influence, financial status, or social media following. We may inflate our own importance or diminish others based on the perceived strength of our intellect or our material possessions. However, all such comparisons are illusory and devoid of truth.

True wisdom lies in transcending these delusions and recognizing the inherent completeness within ourselves and others. When we give or receive, when we interact with the world, we should do so with clarity and awareness, free from the distortions of ego and comparison.

In truth, everything is an expression of wholeness and completeness. When we affirm, "I am Brahman," it is not merely as an individual entity but as an embodiment of that universal completeness. Similarly, every being, every phenomenon, is an expression of the same underlying wholeness. Recognizing this truth, we can liberate ourselves from the illusions of comparison and ego, embracing the boundless unity of existence.

In our journey through life, every action we undertake, every interaction we engage in is rooted in the awareness of wholeness. We give reverence to the Guru or God, draw wisdom from scriptures, nurture disciples, engage in discourse, listen attentively, give generously, and receive humbly—all within the boundless expanse of completeness.

Without this awareness of wholeness, our actions are tainted by illusion. We fall into the trap of hierarchy and comparison, elevating certain figures or realms as superior while denigrating others. We may perceive Krishna, Rama, or other divine beings as inherently superior, or we may idealize concepts of liberation associated with specific traditions or philosophies.

Yet, in truth, all such distinctions are illusory. The essence of Krishna, Rama, and every divine form is inherent within us as expressions of the same universal consciousness. Whether we envision Vaikunta or Kailasha, whether we pursue liberation through devotion or knowledge, it all converges into the singular truth of existence.

"My essence is their essence; their essence is mine"—this realization dissolves the barriers of separation, revealing the interconnectedness of all existence. In this awareness, there is no room for hierarchy or superiority, only the radiant brilliance of unity and completeness.

When we speak of devaluing or elevating, we must recognize the inherent fallacy in such notions. In the grand scheme of existence, there is no concept of diminishing or enhancing the worth of any entity. To illustrate this, consider the analogy of a jewelry shop where diverse ornaments are on display. In this scenario, a dog figurine might hold a higher price tag than an image of Krishna.

If one were to question the shopkeeper about this apparent devaluation of Krishna, the response would be enlightening. The shopkeeper perceives only the intrinsic value of the material—gold—not the outward name or form. Accordingly, the pricing is determined solely by the purity and weight of the gold, not by any perceived significance attached to the forms themselves.

This analogy serves as a poignant reminder of our own illusions and misconceptions. While we may assign varying levels of importance to different forms—be they images of revered deities or ordinary objects—the truth remains unchanged. Just as the gold in the jewelry shop holds inherent value regardless of its form, so too does the essence of all existence possess intrinsic worth.

In this light, whether we encounter images of revered higher beings, divine deities, or fellow humans, we must strive to perceive beyond the superficial distinctions. At the core of every form lies the same essence—the eternal truth of Brahman. As Sat, Chit, Ananda—Existence, Consciousness, Bliss—our nature mirrors the wholeness of the cosmos. Any perceived hierarchy or comparison stems from our own limited perspectives, not from the ultimate reality of unity and completeness.

The allure of limited happiness often captivates us, drawing us into a cycle of fleeting pleasures and inevitable disappointments. However, if we dare to expand our horizons beyond the confines of limitation, we will discover a boundless reservoir of bliss awaiting our embrace. This realm of unlimited joy transcends the petty divisions and conflicts bred by narrow perspectives.

It is the limited view that fuels the fires of discord, igniting wars and perpetuating cycles of suffering. When the mind is ensnared by the illusions of birth and death, it becomes trapped in a turbulent whirlwind of desires and fears. Yet, in the vast expanse of wholeness, such illusions dissolve into insignificance.

Within the realm of completeness, birth and death lose their grip on our consciousness, for they are but transient phenomena in the eternal dance of existence. Here, in the infinite expanse of Being, there is neither beginning nor end—only the timeless flow of unbounded bliss. It is in this expansive awareness that true liberation awaits, transcending the limitations of mortal existence and embracing the infinite splendor of the cosmos.

In the realm of wholeness, there exists a sublime equilibrium where nothing can disturb the eternal flow of completeness. Just as waves rise and fall upon the vast ocean, so too do the myriad phenomena of existence emerge and subside within the boundless expanse of Brahman.

Consider the wave upon the ocean's surface—does it truly experience birth or death? No, for it is but a transient expression of the eternal essence of water. In the same way, when one realizes their true nature as Brahman, they transcend the illusion of individuality and recognize themselves as inseparable from the infinite whole.

The ephemeral nature of the physical body, like the fragile clay pot, may experience cessation and transformation, but the essence that underlies all forms remains untouched. Just as the broken pot does not diminish the substance of the mud from which it was formed, so too does the cessation of bodily functions fail to diminish the eternal essence of Brahman.

In the realm of wholeness, there is no room for loss or gain, desire or anger. Every event and every circumstance is but a fleeting ripple upon the surface of an infinite sea of consciousness. When one embraces this truth, they are liberated from the shackles of illusion, and they abide in the timeless serenity of pure awareness.

So, there exists no hierarchy of attainment—no notion of high or low. Even the most tranquil mind, if rooted in illusion, remains susceptible to disturbance when confronted with life's challenges. The calmness it experiences is but a temporary respite, a fleeting glimpse of peace that dissipates in the face of adversity.

It is only when one recognizes their essential nature as Brahman—beyond the realm of individual experience and mental fluctuations—that true and enduring peace is realized. In this state of profound awareness, the mind remains unperturbed by external circumstances, rooted instead in the unshakable serenity of pure consciousness.

When someone declares, "I am fine" or "I am happy," they unwittingly fall into the trap of illusion. Such statements imply a sense of identification with transient states of being—states that inevitably fluctuate and change. In reality, one's true essence transcends these fleeting experiences of happiness or suffering.

To claim, "I am fine," is to overlook the inherent completeness of one's being. It is to confine oneself within the narrow confines of individual identity, disconnected from the boundless expanse of wholeness. True fulfillment lies not in the pursuit of fleeting emotions but in the realization of one's inherent nature as Brahman—the unchanging substratum of existence.

Similarly, to proclaim, "I am happy" or "I am suffering," is to succumb to the illusion of individual identities—the false dichotomy between pleasure and pain. In truth, both happiness and misery are mere ripples on the surface of the vast ocean of consciousness, which remains untouched by the ebb and flow of worldly experiences.

To transcend the illusion of duality is to abide in the state of Satchitananda—existence, consciousness, and absolute bliss. In this state of profound awareness, one recognizes that their true nature is not bound by the limitations of individual identity or the fluctuations of the mind. Instead, they abide in the eternal truth of wholeness, experiencing the infinite bliss that arises from realizing the oneness of all existence.

To break free from this cycle of illusion, we are guided by the principle of neti neti—negation. Through negation, we strip away the layers of illusion that obscure our understanding, gradually unraveling the fabric of falsehood to reveal the underlying truth.

In reality, all these practices unfold within the same wholeness and completeness. Whether it's our empirical activities or our spiritual endeavors, they are all integral parts of the same, unified whole. Even our acts of devotion and reverence to the God are inseparable from this wholeness.

Therefore, it is essential to transcend the illusion of separation and recognize the inherent unity that underlies all our actions and experiences. By acknowledging the interconnectedness of all practices and experiences, we come to realize the profound oneness that permeates everything.

Hence, God, the scriptures, and the disciple who listens are all expressions of the same wholeness. Within this completeness, there is no room for contradiction or discord. It is only when we stray from this state of wholeness and perceive things in a fragmented manner that we fall into the illusion of bondage.

The True Nature of the Self

We should be clear in our viewpoints. What's the true nature of Self? For an inquiry into this important subject, let us look at the "deep sleep" state, Sushupti. Waking, Dream, and the Deep Sleep States are the three states (most popularly known as Avastha traya) that are most common to every living being in this universe. Everybody invariably experiences these states, and, as such, the deep Sleep state is the 'undifferentiated' state. In this state, there is no awareness of the world around us. There is evādvitīyam brahma. (Ch. Up 6.2.1), "Brahman is one without a second." Exclusive Existence. Interestingly, one is Ekam-One not only in Deep Sleep, but he is Ekam-One in the other two states as well!

How to understand this? We see around us variegated or diversified jivas, individual bodies, and minds in multiplicity. All in pleasures and pains, in hopes and despairs, in utter disorder and chaos, in wars against one another, afflicted by diseases, and so on. How to be free from all these? How to establish order, how to establish happiness, peace in life? Can we observe what's happening here? We are observing all these aspects externally, outwardly, 'para drishti;' something like 'me' and 'not me;' as eternally separate, never destined to meet at all! Whereas in Svadrushti or Atmadrushti, one is All Alone, Satchidananda, Nitya Shuddha Buddha Mukta.

Only in the understanding of the true nature of the Self alone is there a possibility of happiness, peace, etc. It's neither a contract nor a trade, 'you do this. I will liberate you all.' One should note here that the Shrota, the aspirant/ questioner/ listener who is intent on knowing the Truth (Jijnasu), is asking a question quite seriously about his own liberation/freedom from all forms of sorrow and his own welfare (Atmoddhara). So, in reality, there are no fragments in the external world; Mantra says Purnamadah Purnamidam.

Purnamadah, Purnamidam signifies no sense of incompleteness within or without, Vyashti or Samashti in every dimension. Ever fulfilled, Ever peaceful, and Ever free; this being his true nature, the Jijnasu is experiencing bondage, experiencing pairs of pleasures and pains.

One feels subjected to the vagaries of life, tolerating problems. One is targeted by the fits of the anger of others/ or becomes angry at oneself. Therefore, one is seeking freedom from all these. But the catch here is not to seek freedom from anything but to understand the Sruti, which says, 'You are already Ever free.' Sarvam Khalvidam Brahma; all this is Brahman alone; there is nothing other than Brahman. There is only Completeness, and there are no shortcomings whatsoever. However, we first posit that we are insufficient. Then strive or make an effort to fulfill, becoming 'complete.' Thus, a spiritual seeker (Jijnasu) with a mistaken understanding or perception can easily be taken advantage of by others. Alternatively, the seeker may undertake intense spiritual practices such as austerities (tapas), selfless service (Seva), and chanting (Japa), along with various other activities. Despite these efforts, the seeker remains absorbed in these activities without necessarily achieving the intended spiritual clarity or liberation, often due to the initial erroneous perception.

We do not say that such activities are useless. Still, one should realize that they have some limitations in their efficacy and utility. Before one discovers that they are limited in searching for Truth, the 'true' Jijnasu deserves some respite from these activities, which only have a basis in duality and are the outcome of belief in duality. Ultimately, these practices can only take one so far; true realization comes from transcending the dualistic mindset and recognizing the oneness of all existence.

Our Real Nature is Pure Being (Sat Chit Ananda)

The only Truth is SatSwarupa or SwaSwarupa, which is eternal, ever pure, ever potent, and ever-free. So there is no need for any effort in quelling the untruth to find Truth; there is no need for any effort to quell the bondage for freeing oneself. These activities are out of a lack of understanding (Aviveka). The clouds hinder the clear vision of the Sun, whereas the Sun is, by nature, shining brightly on all sides! In the same way, the Ajnani identifies himself as the Jiva in a narrow vision: 'clouds of aviveka hindering clarity. Aviveka is eclipsing the clear vision of the Svarupa. Again, wrongfully projecting all Jivas in the same vision and then putting effort into integrating, thereby hoping to achieve Advaita and hoping to promise Mukti to everyone! Is it not a imagination? Bhavana Advaita? You do this, and I will promise this and this; it's nothing but a trade-in falsehood, not in a real sense. Because one's Svarupa is ever free, this true nature is eclipsed because of Aviveka. So, we think: we are deeply identified with body-mind intellect now. Therefore, we should turn to spirituality and engage in spiritual practices to attain Mukti.

No, we are not talking about bhavanatmaka Mukti. We are talking about Shruti telling: 'You are That'; 'Swatah Siddha Mukta Swarup Brahman You are!' 'But because of inexplicable error (Anirvacaniya Maya), you are misidentifying yourself as body-mind-world complex and believing that falsehood is the only truth.' This is an erroneous perception. But for this misconception, You Are essentially Nitya, Mukta ever free, ever fulfilled (Purnam). Satyam Shivam Sundaram; Ever Real, Ever Shivam means ever Mangala Rupam (ever auspicious), Ever Beautiful. We are not putting any effort here; rather, there is no means to attain or achieve such a goal. It's only Awareness of this reality that is pointed out here.

Don't Give Reality to the False

There can be no true understanding (Samyak Jnana) when we engage in spiritual practices while still believing the world to be ultimately real.

So the first step is to recognize false as false, not real. Because Brahman alone is real, and the world is unreal, appearing as real but genuinely unreal. It's only a 'pratiti' appearance only. That's why it is false, and it's very visible to our eyes but still unreal, as there is no independent existence of its own.

When we have understanding of the Shruti then it is 'Sarvam Khalvidam Brahma' or 'There is nothing else other than Brahman' Nothing is other than Purnatvam- Completeness. That 'Sat' is why we emphasize it here; listen carefully to what is being told here; do not get confused. We are not talking of 'getting you Mukti' or promising anything, saying we will wash your sins and destroy your sins; nothing is promised here either by the Rishis/Upanishads. Dvaita, duality is the outcome of the wrong perception, and it's only our imagination. We set out to rectify it/change it/alter it with a view to getting Mukti. These activities are ill-founded and in vain. Placing reality in what is false and then striving to free oneself from such falsehood—such as desire, anger, and fear (Kama, Krodha, Bhaya)—is contradictory. When false reality is firmly embedded in worldly affairs, extricating oneself becomes impossible. The only way out is through the right understanding that the world is unreal and has no independent existence of its own.

In Svarupa Satya, the true nature of reality, there is only one, with no second entity—no dvitiya. Fear (bhayam) exists only when there is a sense of 'other' or 'second.' How can we create a false sense of the second or third, which doesn't actually exist, and then strive to eliminate them? It is impossible because this false sense was self-created.

The World is in Your Mind

'I have become a renunciate (taken Sanyasa) to get out of this samsara. But, oh man, I must distance myself from this world (Prapancha). This Prapancha is troubling' me'; this type of sanyasa will not free one from samsara. As long as one continues to perceive the world (Prapancha/Samsara) as real (Satyatva buddhi), this world will continue to cause trouble because the belief in its reality fuels these issues. Essentially, one creates these obstacles for oneself. There is no use in blaming others or circumstances, as the perception of reality is the result of one's own erroneous understanding.

So if the key is to remove this falsehood, then only there's 'Samsara Nivriti,' then only there is a possibility of freedom from 'world.' This freedom is only in the right understanding, 'in discernment/Viveka,' not by running away from 'world'! After 'running away to where? What is the place which is not 'the 'world?' Wherever you go, there is this 'world,' and you can not avoid it! The world surrounds you, the world made of Five Great Elements -' Pancha Mahabhutas.'

Once, some 50 years ago, a young man ran away from home to avoid 'worldly things,' as his parents wanted him to get married and settle in life. He belonged to a rich family with good business. But he was in search of something other than worldly things; not sure of what he wanted; something vague, hoping 'liberation,' something like that......He reached somewhere far away in Punjab, where a Sadhu monk spotted him and asked him. "You have run away from home, and you've been wandering here and there aimlessly, looking for the unknown. Have you noticed any sixth bhutA (element) anywhere on your way?" He was clueless and stared blankly at the Sadhu. "It's the 'sixth Element' other than the Five Great Elements? Panch Mahabhu? "No, he replied. What is this sixth one? Upon this, the monk suggested to him, "You are pursuing the unknown, not sure of what it is; it's better to go back to your place and approach your Guru to know what's the Truth. So he came back and narrated the event to his Guru. Muppinarya Swamiji told him, 'what you are seeking' is not to be sought after. It is not a thing of time and space' explained the Swamiji.

He was counseled and told it could not be searched for. We think that the whole world is against us; it's troubling us and deceiving us. The so-called worldly infatuations/attractions drown us. The circumstances are hostile, etc. Therefore, we cannot find Mukthi based on circumstances, favorable or otherwise. It's like hoping to swim in the sea only after the waves subside. The world is like that only, and one cannot change it, rectify it, or alter it. It's like a dog's tail—so stubborn!

The Whole Universe is Yourself

So what is needed is 'the 'Arivu'- understanding, discernment regarding our true nature, Svarupa. One thing is for sure 'We should not place too much 'reality' on names and forms, on transient things.' Ok, but more important is understanding the Svarupa; there is nothing other than this in existence. And that, if anything else is, is the outcome of our imaginations, projections, 'our Sankalpa and vikalpa'; placing reality on transient things is deplorable.

It is not to state that we should not feel 'painful' on being pricked by a needle or knife because the body is mithya, 'unreal.' It is important to note that each organ of our's has its own characteristics, 'svabhava'; they are all bound to react/respond differently in different circumstances/ changes. The body has the quality of growing, wearing, tearing, becoming old, dying, etc. The mind always projects, imagines, doubts; Prana induces thirst and hunger. And so on and on. We can not prevent nor avoid these; these are all-natural tendencies of 'matter.'

These aspects are not negotiable. Physical pain or pleasure are natural phenomena; we are not discussing these things here; we do not

call them "mithya" or 'unreal' in that sense, saying they don't exist like sky flowers. Therefore, they have relevance in the Vyaavahaarika Satya, transactional realm.

What is intended here is that these are called 'Samsara' and are not there in the Self/ Atma / Brahman because Self / Atma / Brahman is totally different from the Body-Mind-Intellect complex. In other words, they are not different from Self-nature the Brahman like waves in water or ornaments in gold. So non-dual means it is all alone, and there is no 'second.'

Vyavaharika Satya, transactional reality, and Paramarthika Satya -Absolute Reality- are two different things at two different levels. Transactional reality is, as per 'Prarabdha', the results of Karmas to be exhausted in the present lifetime. So we are also not talking/discussing 'Prarabdha' here.

What is the right approach to know? What is Sat? This is the core issue. This is the issue the seeker should be earnestly concerned about; you and I should be concerned about it. We should be concerned about 'jIvanmukti,' liberation/ freedom while living, embodied (not after death).

3. Self-Realization

Self-realization represents a profound departure from the pursuit of escapism, which often manifests as a quest for heightened sensations or transient highs induced by substances like drugs or alcohol. Instead, it offers a journey inward, a deep and transformative inquiry into the very nature of the Self—the core of our being. This exploration is not about losing oneself but about discovering and recognizing who we truly are. In the pursuit of self-realization, we embark on an inward odyssey that transcends the superficial allure of sensory indulgence. It is a journey of profound significance that aligns with the ancient lineage of Guru Parampara, a tradition that has passed down timeless wisdom through generations. Central to this wisdom is the potent declaration, 'Tat twam asi'—'You are that.' This statement serves as a beacon guiding seekers towards the recognition of their innate nature, dispelling the misconception that self-realization entails a state of incapacitation or memory loss.

The essence of self-realization lies in self-inquiry—a relentless examination of the Self's true nature. It is an act of turning the spotlight of awareness inward, peeling away the layers of conditioning, beliefs, and false identifications that have accumulated over time. This process is akin to peering into a mirror, not to see a reflection, but to witness the source of reflection itself. Through self-inquiry, we come to realize that we are not limited by our physical bodies, nor are we defined solely by the fluctuations of the mind or the fleeting experiences of the external world. Instead, we uncover an intrinsic and timeless truth—the recognition of our essential nature as consciousness itself. As Gita says in 2:21 vedāvināśhinaṁ nityaṁ, know Atma the Self to be imperishable, eternal, unborn, and immutable.

In this realization, there is no loss of self; rather, there is an unveiling of the authentic Self—the Self that transcends the limitations of the ego and the illusions of separation. It is a profound recognition that we are not mere individuals navigating through life in isolation; we are Being-Knowing-Bliss. Self-realization offers a return to our true essence, a homecoming to the unchanging core of our being. It liberates us from the fleeting highs and lows of the external world and grants access to a profound inner stillness—the wellspring of lasting peace and contentment. Self-realization is not an escape but a courageous and transformative journey into the depths of self-discovery. As Gita says in Verse 10:34 medhā dhṛitiḥ kṣhamā, intelligence, courage, and forgiveness are the qualities an aspirant should have. It is an exploration of the eternal truth that lies beyond the transient sensations of the world. Through self-inquiry, we align with our inherent nature and recognize that, indeed, 'Tat twam asi'—'You are that.' Self-realization is the path to authentic freedom, where we discover that our true nature is not lost but found and that the essence of our being is eternal and boundless.

The Essence of Everyday Existence

In our daily lives, the profound significance of Self-realization becomes evident as we recognize that everything emanates from the ultimate source—the essence of Being-Knowing. This understanding fundamentally alters our perspective on existence. At the core of Self-realization lies the realization that we cannot be anything other than what we truly are. As Gita says in 2:16 nāsato vidyate bhāvo nābhāvo, Of the transient, there is no endurance, and of the eternal, there is no cessation. We are eternally connected to the essence of Being-Knowing, and this connection persists even when we find ourselves momentarily overshadowed by tumultuous emotions such as anger, desire, pride, or arrogance. These emotions, while powerful and often compelling, do not alter our essential nature. They are like passing clouds that momentarily obscure the unchanging radiance of the sun. At times, we succumb to the illusion of individuality, clinging to the belief that we are distinct entities tied to the limitations of the body-mind complex. This delusion leads us to act within the confines of time, where past experiences and future expectations exert their influence.

As a result, our actions become the seeds that yield the fruits of happiness or misery. The outcomes of our actions are depending on our lives, shaped by the circumstances we encounter and driven by the interplay of ignorance, desires, and the actions we take. However, Self-realization guides us beyond the confines of this cyclic existence. It liberates us from the illusion of individuality and reveals the truth that our essential nature is one with the timeless essence of Being-Knowing. It awakens us to the realization that, irrespective of momentary fluctuations in our emotional state or the transient nature of worldly events, our fundamental essence remains unaltered. In this awakened state, we no longer identify exclusively with the body-mind complex but recognize our innate connection to the eternal source of existence.

Our actions cease to be mere reactions to external circumstances or products of desire-driven impulses. Instead, they become expressions of our inherent wisdom, guided by a profound recognition of the essence. Self-realization transforms our everyday lives by revealing the unchanging essence of Being-Knowing as the foundation of our existence. It empowers us to navigate the fluctuations of life with equanimity, recognizing that happiness and misery are transient experiences 2-14 Gita: śhītoṣhṇa-sukha-duḥkha-dāḥ āgamāpāyino anityā. Through self-realization, we awaken to our true nature and embody the wisdom that transcends the dualities of the world, embracing a life of profound harmony and inner peace.

The Dual Nature of Human Existence

In the complex view of human existence, the pursuit of happiness and the desire to escape from misery are dominant threads that weave through our lives. These two states often seem like polar opposites, but in the grand scheme of existence, they are like two faces of the same coin—intimately connected, both arising from the interplay of ignorance and desire. The relentless pursuit of happiness is a universal theme in human life. It drives us to seek joy, pleasure, and contentment in various forms—whether through personal achievements, relationships, material possessions, or fleeting sensory experiences. This pursuit, while natural and deeply ingrained, often leaves us feeling like we are chasing a mirage.

The elusiveness of lasting happiness becomes apparent as we experience fleeting moments of joy followed by the inevitable return of challenges and sorrows. On the flip side, the desire to escape from misery is another prevailing aspect of human existence. Misery takes many forms, from physical pain and emotional suffering to mental anguish and existential angst. It is our natural instinct to avoid or alleviate these states, and we employ various strategies to do so, ranging from seeking external distractions to numbing our pain through substances or unhealthy behaviors. However, the relief is often short-lived, and the misery returns, sometimes even more intensely than before.

These states of happiness and misery are not isolated experiences but are intimately interconnected. They are the dual outcomes of actions born of desire and ignorance. Our desires propel us to act in pursuit of what we believe will bring happiness, and these actions yield results. Depending on various factors, these results can manifest as either happiness or misery. This interplay of desire, action, and consequence creates a self-perpetuating cycle of entanglement, trapping us in a seemingly endless loop.

In wisdom, this cycle of entanglement is often described as the dance of pairs of opposites—where happiness and misery, pleasure and pain, success and failure are inextricably linked. The pursuit of one side of the duality inevitably leads to the experience of the other, and so the cycle continues. Breaking free from this cycle requires a shift in perspective—a transcendence of the dualities that bind us. As Gita says in verse 2:38 sukha-duḥkhe same kṛitvā, treating alike happiness and misery, it involves recognizing that both happiness and misery are transient, impermanent states. They are like passing clouds in the vast sky of our consciousness.

True liberation comes not from incessantly pursuing one side of the duality or seeking to escape from the other but from understanding the nature of desire and ignorance themselves. In the light of self-awareness and wisdom, we come to see that the pursuit of lasting happiness is not found in external circumstances or fleeting pleasures but in the recognition of our inherent wholeness and inner peace.

Similarly, the escape from misery is not achieved by avoiding pain but by understanding the roots of suffering and finding inner resilience. In essence, the dual nature of human existence serves as a powerful catalyst for self-discovery and spiritual growth. It prompts us to inquire into the nature of desire, the workings of the mind, and the essence of our true selves. Ultimately, it is through this inner journey of self-realization that we can transcend the cycle of entanglement and find a profound and lasting sense of fulfillment beyond the ever-shifting tides of happiness and misery.

Breaking Free from the Cycle of Dualities

Our journey is one often marked by the relentless pursuit of happiness while simultaneously seeking refuge from the clutches of misery. These two states appear as distinct, even opposing facets of existence. However, when we peer deeper into the intricate fabric of life, we uncover a profound truth—happiness and misery are not isolated entities but are intricately connected, both arising from the interplay of desire and ignorance.

This understanding, though profound, poses a formidable challenge. Breaking free from the cycle of dualities, where happiness and misery seem to hold sway over our consciousness, can feel like an undefeatable task. These emotional states often exert such overpowering influence that they render us incapacitated, dictating the course of our lives. The entanglement in this cycle is not a mere accident or individual misfortune; it is an intrinsic aspect of the human condition. It is woven into the very fabric of the world we inhabit, shaping our experiences, actions, and reactions. It is a reflection of the intricate dance between our desires and our ignorance, a dance that plays out on the stage of existence.

Desire, a fundamental aspect of the human psyche, propels us forward in our pursuit of happiness. It drives us to seek joy, pleasure, and contentment in various forms, from personal achievements to relationships, material possessions, and sensory experiences. This pursuit is deeply ingrained, an integral part of our nature. However, it often feels like chasing a mirage, as the happiness we seek remains elusive and fleeting. Simultaneously, the desire to escape from misery arises as a natural instinct. Misery encompasses physical pain, emotional suffering, mental anguish, and existential questions that weigh heavily on our hearts and minds. When faced with these forms of suffering, we yearn for relief and employ various strategies to alleviate our pain. Yet, the respite is often brief, and the misery returns, sometimes with even greater intensity.

Gita 3:39, āvṛitaṁ jñānam etena jñānino nitya-vairiṇā kāma-rūpeṇa, Desire, in the form of an insatiable and relentless fire, acts as a constant adversary to those who seek true knowledge and wisdom. It shrouds the brilliance of knowledge with its veil, obscuring the path to self-realization. The wise individual, well-acquainted with the nature of desire, recognizes its capacity to lead one astray. Even before desire can entice him into unwise actions, he senses its presence and experiences inner turmoil. This discerning awareness causes distress in the wise, as they understand the potential consequences of succumbing to desire. In contrast, the fool perceives desire as a friend while it lasts, viewing it as a source of pleasure and gratification. It is only when sorrow and suffering inevitably follow in desire's wake that the fool realizes the detrimental effects. However, this realization comes too late, after the damage has been done.

Desire, thus, becomes the relentless enemy of the wise, perpetually lurking in the form of insatiable longing and an unquenchable fire. It is this desire that veils the path to true knowledge and wisdom, and the wise individual must constantly strive to overcome its influence in their pursuit of self-realization and inner peace. Understanding the abode of this enemy, the wise can work towards taming and ultimately transcending the relentless desires that hinder their spiritual journey. The cycle of dualities, the relentless dance between happiness and misery, is an intricate web that ensnares us. It can feel like an inescapable trap, as the pendulum swings between pleasure and pain, success and failure, and joy and sorrow. This entanglement is not a personal failing but a shared human experience, a universal thread that binds us together in the essence of existence.

So, Gita says 4:40 na sukhaṁ sanśhayātmanaḥ, Happiness comes with Self-knowledge, but doubt erases joy, in this world and in the next. So, banish doubt, embrace Self-realization. So, breaking free from this cycle requires a shift in consciousness, a transcendence of the dualities that bind us. It involves recognizing that both happiness and misery are impermanent, transitory states. They are like passing clouds in the vast expanse of our consciousness.

Liberation does not come from relentlessly pursuing one side of the duality or seeking to evade the other; it arises from understanding the very nature of desire and ignorance themselves. In this journey of self-discovery and awakening, we come to see that lasting happiness is not found in external circumstances or fleeting pleasures but in the recognition of our inherent wholeness and inner peace. Similarly, freedom from misery is not attained by avoiding pain but by understanding the roots of suffering and cultivating inner resilience. So, breaking free from the entanglement of dualities is indeed a formidable challenge. Yet, it is a challenge that invites us to embark on a profound inner journey—a journey of self-realization and wisdom. Through this journey, we can transcend the cycle of dualities and discover a profound and enduring sense of fulfillment that goes beyond the ever-shifting tides of happiness and misery.

The Path to Transcending Dualities

In the phenomenon of human existence, the ceaseless pursuit of happiness and the desire to escape from misery often dominate our lives. However, the solution to transcending this perpetual cycle lies in a profound shift of perception—a recognition of the transitory nature of these emotional states. True happiness, the kind that remains unshaken by the vicissitudes of life, is not to be found in the ephemeral. The pursuit of fleeting pleasures, momentary gratifications, and external achievements may offer temporary respite, but it is akin to chasing a mirage in the desert. The happiness that arises from such pursuits is illusory, like a child's fear of ghosts lurking beneath the bed. In the darkness of ignorance, we often believe that these fleeting moments of pleasure represent the pinnacle of happiness. We seek them relentlessly, convinced that they hold the key to our well-being. Yet, like the child who fears the imaginary specter, we are entrapped in a web of illusion.

The experience of happiness is undoubtedly real; it is a genuine facet of human life. However, it dissipates upon close scrutiny and proper inquiry. When we turn our attention inward and examine the nature of our desires and the objects of our pursuit, we begin to unravel the illusion. We come to realize that the happiness derived from external sources is transient and conditional. It is subject to the ever-changing circumstances of life, often dependent on external factors that lie beyond our control. This realization is like lifting the bed sheet and discovering that there are no ghosts hiding underneath—only the play of shadows and imagination.

Gita 18:38, vishayendriya-sanyogād yat tad agre 'mṛitopa-mampariṇāme viṣham iva tat sukhaṁ rājasaṁ smṛitam. The joy that arises from the contact of the senses with their objects is initially sweet, resembling nectar in its early moments. However, this pleasure, born of the restless quality of rajas, takes on a deceptive character. In the end, it transforms into something bitter, akin to poison. It leads to a loss of physical and mental strength, wisdom, and inner beauty. Moreover, it erodes one's retentive faculties, wealth, and diligence. Ultimately, this pleasure is the root cause of vice and its attendant suffering, leading individuals away from the path of true fulfillment and self-realization.

Through self-inquiry and introspection, we begin to discern that true and enduring happiness is not contingent on external conditions or fleeting sensory pleasures. It arises from an inner source, a deep wellspring of contentment that transcends the dualities of the external world. As we recognize the transitory nature of happiness, we also come to understand the imperma-nence of misery. Just as happiness arises and subsides, so too does suffering. The pains and sorrows that we seek to escape are not eternal tormentors, but passing clouds in the sky of our consciousness.

Gita 18:37, yat tad agre viṣham iva pariṇāme 'mṛitopamamtat sukhaṁ sāttvikaṁ proktam ātma-buddhi-prasāda-jam. The joy that resembles poison in its early stages, marked by struggle in acquiring knowledge, detachment, and meditation, ultimately transforms into nectar-like bliss in its mature phase. This transformation arises from the purity and clarity of one's intellect, which is deeply connected with the Self. Such joy is classified as sattvik, born of the quality of sattva, according to the wisdom of the learned. It is the sublime and enduring joy that springs from the harmony of self-realization and inner clarity. This recognition empowers us to approach both happiness and misery with equanimity. We no longer cling desperately to the fleeting highs, nor do we fear the lows. Instead, we navigate the dualities of life with a serene understanding that both joy and sorrow are transient visitors.

The path to transcending the cycle of misery and happiness lies in recognizing their impermanent nature. True and enduring happiness is not to be found in the external world but arises from within. It is a realization that liberates us from the illusion of chasing shadows and allows us to embrace the profound and unchanging contentment that resides at the core of our being. Through this recognition, we find liberation from the ever-spinning wheel of dualities, stepping into the realm of lasting inner peace.

Liberation from Cyclic Limitations

The ceaseless cycle of happiness and misery that we often find ourselves entangled in eventually becomes constraining and limiting. It is as if we are caught in a perpetual loop from which escape seems elusive. Gita 9:3 mṛityu-samsāra-vartmani, repeatedly come back to this world in the cycle of birth and death.

However, within this cycle, the teachings of Sruti, the sacred scriptures, emerge as a guiding light, beckoning us toward a profound awakening—a realization of our true nature and the dissolution of this perpetual cycle. The teachings of Sruti are not mere words on a page but profound revelations that have been passed down through generations. These sacred scriptures carry the wisdom of ages, and when embraced with an open heart and a receptive mind, they become a transformative force in our lives. In the throes of this cyclic existence, the teachings of Sruti serve as a powerful reminder that we are not composed of the fleeting emotions, desires, and attachments that often dictate our actions and reactions. Instead, they point us toward a deeper reality—an inherent freedom that transcends the ebb and flow of emotions.

These teachings introduce us to our true nature, unveiling the timeless truth that resides within us. They peel away the layers of illusion, inviting us to recognize our essential nature as Being-Knowing. It is as if a veil of ignorance is gradually lifted, allowing the radiant light of awareness to dispel the darkness of delusion. As we immerse ourselves in the wisdom of Sruti, we begin to understand that our identity is not confined to the ever-changing landscape of thoughts and emotions. We come to realize that beneath the turbulence of the mind, there exists a serene and unchanging essence—a state of pure awareness.

As Kena says in Mantra 1: verse 2, śrotrasya śrotram manaso mano, Self is the ear of the ear, the mind of the mind. This awakening is not a mere intellectual exercise but a profound shift in our perception of reality. It is an experiential revelation that transcends the limitations of words and concepts. In the light of this awareness, the cycle of happiness and misery loses its grip on us. We no longer identify exclusively with the fluctuations of pleasure and pain, for we have touched upon a reality that remains untouched by the dualities of the world. The teachings of Sruti guide us toward the recognition of our ultimate freedom—the freedom to transcend the cyclic limitations of existence. Through understanding and realization, we come to embody the truth that we are not bound by the relentless cycle but are, in fact, the eternal essence of Being-Knowing. This profound revelation is not a destination but a continuous journey of self-discovery, where the light of awareness forever dispels the shadows of ignorance.

Actions in the Light of Awareness

In the realm of self-realization, actions take on a profoundly different quality. They unfold not as means to dull the mind or seek sensory highs, as is often the case in the ordinary pursuit of life, but rather as expressions of an unwavering awareness—a profound recognition of the transitory nature of all experiences.

naiva kiñchit karomīti yukto manyeta tattva-vitpaśhyañ
śhriṇvan spṛiśhañjighrann aśhnangachchhan
svapañśhvasanpralapan visṛijan gṛihṇann unmiṣhan
nimiṣhann apiindriyāṇīndriyārtheṣhu vartanta iti dhārayan

Remaining absorbed in the Self, the knower of Reality should think, 'I certainly do not do anything,' even while seeing, hearing, touching, smelling, eating, moving, sleeping, breathing, speaking, releasing, holding, opening, and closing the eyes—remembering that the organs function in relation to the objects of the organs.

Gita: 5: 8-9

In this state of heightened consciousness, we become acutely aware that sensations, perceptions, feelings, and thoughts are ephemeral. They arise and fade away like ripples on the surface of a pond. In this awareness, we recognize a deeper essence that remains untouched by the transient dance of life's fluctuations. It is akin to perceiving the pure gold that lies beneath the various forms and appearances of ornaments. This discernment is not a mere intellectual understanding; it is a direct experiential realization. It is as if we have moved from being entangled within the web of our sensory experiences to becoming a silent observer—a witness to the ever-changing panorama of life.

In this state of heightened awareness, we are not overwhelmed by the passing currents of pleasure and pain. Instead, we remain rooted in the unchanging essence of our being. Our actions cease to be driven by the insatiable desires of the ego but flow from a place of inner stillness and wisdom. Dispassion naturally permeates all our daily activities. It is not a forced renunciation of the world but a natural outcome of realizing that the pursuit of external stimuli can never quench the deep yearning for lasting contentment. We recognize that the true source of fulfillment lies not in the external world but within ourselves. Every transaction, every interaction, and every moment becomes an opportunity to live as awareness. Whether we are engaged in our professions, nurturing relationships, or simply going about our daily routines, the radiance of the Self shines through.

In this awakened state, our actions are no longer driven by the need to acquire or achieve. Instead, they are infused with a sense of purpose that transcends personal gain. Self-realization transforms our approach to actions and daily life. It shifts the focus from the pursuit of fleeting sensory pleasures to the cultivation of unwavering awareness. In this state, the radiance of the Self blossoms, and every moment becomes an opportunity for profound inner fulfillment and the expression of profound love and compassion.

The Quest for Self-Realization

In the profound journey of self-realization, certain questions emerge as guiding beacons, illuminating the path to understanding our true nature. Questions such as "Who am I?" and "What is my relationship to the world?" take on profound significance. They become essential inquiries that prompt us to delve into the depths of our existence, exploring the possibilities of attaining true freedom and understanding when such freedom can be realized. These questions, seemingly simple yet infinitely profound, emerge from the very heart of human experience. They arise not from the shallowness of curiosity but from the depths of our soul's longing for truth and liberation. They are inquiries that challenge the conventional understanding of our identity and the nature of our connection to the world.

"Who am I?" is a question that pierces through the layers of conditioning, roles, and identities that we accumulate throughout our lives. It prompts us to examine the core of our being—the essence that transcends the ever-changing roles we play in society, the labels we adopt, and the masks we wear. It is an inquiry that leads us to recognize that our true identity is not confined to the body-mind complex but is a timeless and unchanging reality.

"What is my relationship to the world?" delves into the intricacies of our interconnectedness with the external universe. It invites us to explore the web of relationships, responsibilities, and interactions that define our lives. This question challenges us to move beyond the surface-level understanding of separateness and isolation, revealing a profound interdependence that binds us to the fabric of existence. These questions do not arise from a place of knowledge or understanding but from the recognition of our ignorance—the ignorance of the Self, which is the ultimate reality. It is this ignorance that veils our true nature and keeps us entangled in the dualities of the world—happiness and misery, success and failure, pleasure and pain. The quest for self-realization begins with these questions as its foundation. They serve as the initial spark that ignites the journey of self-inquiry—a journey that leads us from darkness to light, from confusion to clarity, and from bondage to freedom.

Through contemplation and introspection, we begin to unravel the layers of ignorance that obscure our innate wisdom.

.As we explore these questions and peel away the layers of conditioning and false identifications, we come face to face with the profound truth—the truth of our essential nature as pure consciousness, unbound by time and space. We recognize that the egoic self, with its desires and fears, is but a temporary construct, while the true Self is eternal and unchanging. .The answers to these questions do not lie in mere words or concepts but in direct experiential realization. They are not intellectual exercises but transformative journeys that lead us to the innermost core of our being. It is in the light of this realization that the ignorance of the Self is dispelled and the radiance of truth shines forth.

> yo māṁ paśhyati sarvatra sarvaṁ cha mayi paśhyati
> tasyāhaṁ na pranaśhyāmi sa cha me na pranaśhyati

> One who perceives Me, 'I', as the Self within all beings
> and sees all things, from the smallest to the greatest,
> as existing in Me, does not lose their connection to
> Me. Likewise, I, as the ultimate seer of the unity of the
> Self in all, do not lose sight of such a realized soul.
>
> Gita 6:30

This profound identity between the individual and the Divine ensures an unbreakable bond, for what is truly one's own Self is held dearly and eternally within the vision of the Supreme. So, questions like "Who am I?" and "What is my relationship to the world?" are the signposts on the path to self-realization. They emerge from the recognition of our ignorance and lead us toward the ultimate truth—the realization of the Self as the ultimate reality. Through contemplation and self-inquiry, we embark on a profound journey of self-discovery, where the answers to these questions become the keys to unlocking the door to lasting freedom and understanding.

Gurus and Sruti

In the profound journey of self-realization, the lineage and role of spiritual guides, or gurus, and the wisdom of Sruti, the sacred scriptures, is paramount. They serve as beacons of light, guiding us to a deeper understanding of our connection to the world. Their teachings emphasize a fundamental truth—that we are not mere individual body-mind complexes but something far more profound and expansive. The teachings of gurus and the wisdom of Sruti resonate with declarations such as "You are that Self," "You are that essence," "You are that being-knowing," and "You are that Brahman." These statements are not mere words but profound pointers to our essential nature. They direct our attention away from the limited identification with the body-mind complex and towards the recognition of our true identity.

The journey towards this realization begins with the fundamental question, "Who am I?" It is a question that carries the weight of centuries of wisdom and spiritual inquiry. It is a question that cuts through the layers of conditioning, illusion, and ignorance that have accumulated over the course of our lives. It prompts us to look beyond the surface-level roles and identities we assume and seek the essence of our being. The significance of this question lies in the recognition that, even though we are that ultimate reality, we remain unaware of it. We have mistaken ourselves for the transient and ever-changing body-mind complex, a misconception perpetuated by our day-to-day experiences and societal conditioning.

The journey of self-realization is, therefore, an awakening of awareness—a profound realization that our inherent nature cannot be altered simply because we have misidentified ourselves. Gurus, who have themselves traversed the path of self-realization, play a pivotal role in facilitating this awakening of awareness. They serve as guides and mentors, illuminating the path and offering insights garnered from their own inner journeys. Their wisdom is not theoretical but experiential, a living testament to the profound transformation that is possible through self-inquiry.

The teachings of Sruti, the sacred scriptures, complement the guidance of gurus. They provide a timeless and universal framework for understanding the nature of reality and the self. These scriptures, often transmitted through oral tradition, contain profound revelations and the ultimate reality that underlies the manifest world. Together, the teachings of gurus and the wisdom of Sruti create a synergy that propels seekers on the path of self-realization. They offer a road map for transcending the limited and illusory identification with the body-mind complex and recognizing the unchanging and eternal essence that dwells within. The awakening of awareness is not a one-time event but a continuous journey. It involves a shift in perspective—from seeing ourselves as separate individuals to recognizing absolute reality. It requires a willingness to question our assumptions, challenge our conditioning, and explore the depths of our own consciousness.

> brahma vā idamagra āsīt, tadātmānamevāvet,
> aham brahmāsmīti
>
> Brihadaranyaka Upanishad 1.4.10

The essence of this teaching is that Atma, the Self was, from the very beginning, the Supreme Brahman. It affirms that the eternal truth is "I am Brahman." Every individual, inherently one with Brahman, is fundamentally identical with all of existence. However, ignorance casts a veil, superimposing the mistaken notion that one is not Brahman and not part of the unified whole. This distortion is akin to mistaking a mother-of-pearl for silver or imagining the limitless sky as concave or blue.The knowledge of Brahman serves as the remedy, dispelling the illusion of separateness and restoring the recognition of the inherent unity. Therefore, it is entirely appropriate to affirm that what was originally and fundamentally the Supreme Brahman is referred to in the statement, "This was indeed Brahman in the beginning."

This interpretation aligns with the primary and authentic meaning of the term "Brahman" in the Vedas. It is crucial not to misconstrue the word "Brahman" here as representing a person who will become Brahman in the future, as this contradicts its intended meaning. The teachings of the Śruti emphasize adhering to the plain and original sense of a term used in the scriptures, unless there is a profound and purposeful reason to attribute a different interpretation. In this case, the ultimate truth is that the self has always been and will forever be the Supreme Brahman. Gurus and Sruti are guiding lights on the path of self-realization. They remind us that we are not limited to the transient experiences of the body-mind complex but are the vast, unbounded essence of existence. The fundamental question of "Who am I?" serves as the gateway to this profound realization—a realization that liberates us from the shackles of ignorance and leads us to the boundless truth of our essential nature.

Recognizing the Vastness of Our True Essence

In the dominance of human existence, our day-to-day experiences often lead us to believe that we are confined within the boundaries of the body-mind-world complex. It is a perspective deeply ingrained in our consciousness, a perspective that suggests that we are limited to the transient and ever-changing aspects of our lives. However, there exists a profound objection to this limited perspective—an objection that emerges from the wisdom of Sruti, the sacred scriptures. Sruti asserts that we cannot confine the whole truth to the perspective of a single aspect alone, just as the vastness of the ocean cannot be reduced to the viewpoint of a single wave. This assertion challenges the conventional understanding of our identity and the nature of reality itself. It beckons us to look beyond the surface-level experiences and recognize that our true essence extends far beyond the limitations of the body-mind-world complex. The body-mind-world complex is an intricate web of experiences, perceptions, sensations, thoughts, and emotions. It is a world in which we navigate through the dualities of pleasure and pain, success and failure, and joy and sorrow. While this complex is undeniably a part of our lived reality, it is not the entirety of reality itself.

The objection raised by Sruti is a profound one—it invites us to transcend the confines of our everyday experiences and explore the deeper dimensions of our existence. It challenges the notion that we are defined solely by the roles we play, the labels we adopt, and the identities we assume. Our true essence, as illuminated by the wisdom of Sruti, is not bound by the limitations of time, space, or circumstance. It is a timeless and boundless reality—an essence that transcends the ebb and flow of the external world. It is an unchanging and eternal witness to the ever-changing play of existence.

To grasp this truth, we must shift our perspective. We must move beyond the surface-level identification with the body-mind-world complex and recognize the deeper substratum of our being. This recognition does not negate our experiences; rather, it invites us to see them in a broader context. Our experiences, sensations, perceptions, and emotions are like ripples on the surface of a vast and tranquil lake. They come and go, rise and fall, but the essence of the lake remains unchanged.

Similarly, our true essence remains untouched by the transient fluctuations of the external world. This understanding is not a denial of our experiences but a transcendence of their limitations. It is an awakening to the profound truth that our identity is not confined to the roles we play or the circumstances we encounter. It is a recognition that, beneath the ever-changing surface, there is an unchanging and eternal essence—the essence of our true Self.

Brihadaranyaka Upanishad 4.3.1 yatsākṣādaparokṣādbrahma, the Brahman that is immediate and direct—the Self that is within all. "This is your self that is within all," carries a profound significance. The qualification "that is within all" encompasses all possible qualifications without exception. It refers to the Self in its immediate and unobstructed essence, used in its primary and direct sense. This Self is none other than Brahman, the vastest and all-encompassing reality, the very essence of everything, dwelling within all beings. The vision intrinsic to the Self is analogous to the heat and light emanating from fire. It is the essence of the witnessing consciousness, unbounded by either a beginning or an end. In contrast, ordinary vision is colored by the objects perceived through the eyes and is bound by a definite origin. It can be seen as a reflection of the eternal vision of the Self, and its existence is pervaded by the ever-present witness within.

The eternal vision of the Self is metaphorically referred to as the "witness" because, although it eternally beholds, it is sometimes described as though it sees and sometimes as though it does not. In truth, the vision of the seer, the Self, remains unchanging and eternal, transcending the dualities of seeing and not seeing, and it is the ultimate source of all perception and awareness. The objection raised by Sruti challenges us to expand our perspective and recognize the vastness of our true essence. While the body-mind-world complex is an experience, it is not the entirety of reality. We are invited to move beyond the limitations of this complex and embrace the timeless and boundless truth that resides within us—a truth that transcends the ever-shifting tides of our daily existence.

Realizing Our True Nature

The journey of self-realization takes us on a profound exploration of our true nature, and in this exploration, the body-mind-world complex serves as a unique portal—an entry point into perceiving the whole truth. While our experiences within this complex are transient and ever-changing, the essence that underlies them remains unaltered and eternal. This essence, often referred to as being-knowing, is not an abstract concept but a palpable reality that permeates every cognitive experience. It is the witness to all that unfolds within the intricate web of sensations, perceptions, thoughts, and emotions.

This witness, unchanging and ever-present, is not limited to the individual but extends to the very fabric of existence itself. The body-mind-world complex, with all its complexities and intricacies, provides the canvas upon which the drama of life unfolds. It is the stage where the dualities of pleasure and pain, success and failure, and joy and sorrow play out. Yet, within this ever-shifting theater of existence, the essence remains steady and unwavering. Every experience, whether mundane or extraordinary, arises and subsides. Sensations arise, are felt, and eventually fade away. Perceptions come into being, are known, and dissolve into the background. Thoughts emerge, are recognized, and dissolve into the vastness of consciousness. Emotions surge, are acknowledged, and dissipate like passing clouds.

Amidst this constant flux, the being-knowing essence stands as the unchanging backdrop—a silent observer to the ceaseless dance of existence. It is not an active participant in the drama but the silent witness that enables the drama to unfold. It is the light that illuminates the stage, allowing the actors (experiences) to perform their roles. The realization of this essence is not merely a solution to personal problems or a means of seeking relief from suffering. It is a profound awakening of awareness regarding our true nature and the nature of everything that exists. It invites us to recognize the ever-free essence that underlies all of existence, transcending the limitations of time, space, and circumstance. In this realization, we come to understand that our individuality, our identification with the body-mind complex, is a temporary and illusory veil that obscures the radiant truth of our being.

The essence of being-knowing is not confined to the boundaries of individuality but is the very essence of all that is. It is the common thread that unites us with the entirety of existence, Bhagavad Gita:7:7 sūtre maṇi-gaṇā iva; As we delve deeper into this understanding, we begin to live from a place of profound awareness. We no longer allow the transient experiences of pleasure and pain to dictate the course of our lives. Instead, we navigate the complexities of the world with a sense of detachment and equanimity. So, realizing our true nature involves using the body-mind-world complex as a portal—a gateway to perceiving the whole truth. It is an awakening to the unchanging essence of being-knowing that underlies all experiences. This realization is not a mere intellectual concept but a lived experience that transforms our relationship with the world. It is an invitation to recognize the ever-free essence that permeates all of existence, inviting us to live in alignment with the boundless truth of our being.

karmanaiva hi sansiddhim āsthitā janakādayaḥ
loka-saṅgraham evāpi sampaśhyan kartum arhasi
yad yad ācharati śhreshṭhas tat tad evetaro janaḥ
sa yat pramāṇaṁ kurute lokas tad anuvartate -
Bhagavad Gita 3:20 & 21

King Janaka and others attained perfection by action.
Even having in view the need to show the right
path to the masses, you should work. Whatsoever

a great man does, that other men do; whatever he
sets up as the standard, that the world follows.

In the ancient times, learned individuals like King Janaka and
others, including King Asvapati, were deeply committed to the
pursuit of Liberation or spiritual enlightenment. They recognized that one could attain Liberation through their actions
themselves, meaning that they could continue to engage in
worldly actions while remaining established in the state of
spiritual realization. If we consider that these great beings had
already achieved the highest level of spiritual realization, it
implies that they maintained their connection with worldly
actions. They did not do this for their own sake but rather as a
conscious choice to set an example for others. By continuing to
perform actions, they demonstrated that it was possible to live
in the world while remaining spiritually enlightened.

This was done with the intention of guiding and inspiring
others on the spiritual path. In essence, their actions were not
driven by personal desires or attachment but were a means to
serve as role models and prevent humanity from straying away
from the spiritual path. They showed that one could live in the
world, fulfill their responsibilities, and still be rooted in the
awareness of their true nature and the pursuit of Liberation.
Their actions were selfless and aimed at benefiting society and
helping others on their spiritual journeys.

If we consider that Janaka and other great individuals of
ancient times had not yet attained the fullest realization, then
the verse can be understood in a different light. In this interpretation, it suggests that they gradually became established
in Liberation through their actions. These actions served as a
means for the purification of their minds and hearts. In this
context, their obligatory duties and actions were seen as tools
for inner transformation. Through the performance of their
duties with dedication and a sense of selflessness, they were

able to gradually purify their minds and align them with higher spiritual truths. As they continued to engage in their worldly responsibilities, their actions became a form of spiritual practice, leading them toward a state of Liberation. This perspective highlights the transformative power of selfless and dedicated actions when performed with a sense of duty and without attachment to the fruits of those actions. Even individuals who may not have initially attained full realization can gradually progress on the spiritual path through the purification of their minds and hearts, ultimately leading to Liberation.

The verse emphasizes that the duty of performing actions does not have to be delegated to someone else who has already attained the highest level of enlightenment and reached their spiritual goal. Instead, it addresses the individual who is still under the influence of past actions, which necessitate the performance of duties. In this context, "you" (referring to the individual) are encouraged to fulfill your responsibilities and carry out your duties. Even though you may not have reached the pinnacle of spiritual enlightenment, it is essential to continue performing your duties. However, this should not be done solely as a matter of routine or personal gain. Rather, it should be done with the awareness of the greater purpose, which is the welfare and guidance of humanity. By carrying out your responsibilities and obligations while keeping in mind the well-being and spiritual guidance of others, you contribute to the betterment of society. You become an example for others to follow, demonstrating how one can live a balanced life while progressing on the spiritual path. In this way, you not only fulfill your own duties but also play a role in preventing others from losing their way on the spiritual journey. Your actions become a source of inspiration and guidance for those around you, serving a higher purpose beyond personal advancement.

This verse conveys the principle that the actions of a superior person or a leader serve as a guiding example for others to follow. When a superior individual engages in a particular action, those who look up to them and follow their lead also perform the same action. This is a natural tendency among people, especially when they have respect and admiration for the superior person. Furthermore, the verse suggests that whatever principles or authorities the superior person upholds and follows, the common people also tend to accept and follow those same principles or authorities. It can include both spiritual and worldly matters. The influence of the superior person's actions and beliefs has a profound impact on the behavior and values of the broader community. In the context of the teaching, Lord Krishna encourages Arjuna not to doubt the importance of his role in preventing people from straying from the right path. He essentially tells Arjuna that if he has any doubts regarding his duty in guiding and setting an example for the people, he should observe the Lord himself. Lord Krishna's actions and teachings exemplify the highest moral and spiritual values, serving as a model for Arjuna and all who seek guidance. By following such a role model, individuals can ensure that their actions align with righteousness and contribute positively to society.

Detachment - Go beyond earthly identifications

We should go beyond worldly identifications such as a position, a title, or a rank by mentally giving them up using the neti neti (not this, not this) method. Why should we mentally give them up? Because they are all related to the body and not to the Self, and they only strengthen the 'I am the body' idea. Do we enhance our spiritual knowledge on becoming a resident of an ashram or a sanyAsa or the head of an ashram? Do all sorrows end automatically?

'Promotion' Upgradations' should mean rewarding: reward for efficiency, for good conduct, obedience-commitment-sincerity (to the Self, the consciousness) surrender, Ananya devotion (to the master), capability for shouldering higher responsibilities with courage (for the World) and of all SELF SACRIFICE, etc., These are all fine, deserve compliments! But suppose a couple of these are missing or are founded on erroneous footing/ foundation? Then, the castle of cards will collapse and crash down with the slightest push/wind!

However, during some adverse situations, one collapses, slips from control, and becomes a target of one's own anger, desires, hatred, arrogance, jealousy, miseries, agonies, or becomes a target to other's adverse emotions/feelings and gives in to traps of emotional bankruptcy.

Why so? This is surely the outcome of pseudo-control, misplaced/ false self-esteem (mithya- Abhiman) hidden in the corner of the mind, which flares up suddenly. All these shortcomings were so far hidden, suppressed without the right understanding.

So the Advaita teaching is essentially internal, inwardly blossoming of the Lotus of the entire Being founded on the right understanding of the SELF, ATMA THE BRAHMAN, which is Existence-Consciousness-Bliss. It's surely not for public display. Thus spoke Nijaguna Shivayogi, 15th Century King-Saint from Karnataka.

Discriminate Between the Real and the UnReal

The most significant impediment in knowing the Swarupa is our inability to distinguish between Atma and Anatma. This is because we are conditioned to 'objectify' everything in this universe. Everything is an 'object', and that 'object' separates from me, objectification of everything. Like the Hamsa bird, we do not have the right discernment, which takes only the milk and discards water. That 'Viveka' is required, which is true, which is not true.

Body, Mind, and the world around us need to be treated as unreal / mithya because they do not have an independent existence of their own. Waves in the sea would have been 'real' if they had an independent existence of their own. And if we were able to separate or differentiate from the water! If anyone claims that the waves are separate or different from water, then their 'reality'', 'existence,' becomes suspect. Waves are there because water is there. Without water, waves can not be. Still, most of us raise our eyebrows and exclaim, 'how is it? The waves in the sea are unreal? We see them, touch them, feel them, they are visible so clearly? and so on 'how is it that they are unreal.' That's why we are saying they do not have an independent existence of their own! They 'depend' on something (which we call 'substratum') for their existence; in this sense, they must understand the differentiation. So, here, Mitya means it is not totally non-existent like sky flower.

Our Real Nature is Bliss Itself (Ananda)

We are talking about the Bhuma svarupa, Blissful State. Bliss is Svarupa Sukha. If we once understood the Svarupa Sukha (bliss-nature), we will know all sukha. If not, we will struggle with external pleasures that necessarily entail pain. Because all appearances are unreal and are incapable of giving everlasting happiness.

Bliss is nothing but inner-Self, (Pratyak Atma), meaning inwardly directed, internal, directed towards Self. The Self, the Svaswarupa (one's nature) itself, is characterized by Ananda, the Bliss exclusiveness, not the material happiness. The Self in Itself, is the Atma and is Bliss alone. We reject all types of differentiation, negate all types of duality here, and move towards oneness, which is Svarupa. What we call the Bliss is the Svarupa only. Do not be confused here! Bliss is intrinsic in nature, not the outcome of action or inaction. Nor as the enjoyer/sufferer (of results of action).

So its Bliss of exclusivity (Kevala) can be compared to the Deep Sleep state, where all forms of differentiation are completely dissolved. Bliss is not in the forms of pleasure/pains, hopes/despairs, etc. The path towards spirituality is towards Bliss, i.e., complete Bliss, Svarupa Ananda; what is meant here is Eternal Bliss.

So, the path of spirituality should aim at Bliss, total Bliss. Where to find this? In One-Self. This will liberate one from all forms of misery/sorrow. Why this misery/sorrow, because one is searching outside / outwards, from the body-mind world, etc. There is no real existence for the Body-Mind-World complex. So, naturally, it follows that there would never be real happiness in these worldly transient things.

One can come to know about this only by tatva jnana; tatva-Principle; jnana-Knowledge. Then only there is a possibility of total cessation of misery/sorrow (Atyantika Dukha NIvrutti), leading to a Blissful state.

It does not mean that the world is full of misery/sorrow alone. Misery/sorrow is mainly the outcome of our erroneous perception; we have placed reality in 'unreal,' transient things. Thus identifying ourselves with these 'unreal' things and ignoring our True Nature as that of Nitya-shuddha-buddha-mukta.

What is the Truth is: Self alone, Svarupa alone, which is Blissful, Satchidananda (Existence-Consciousness -Bliss). Therefore, the complete elimination of misery/sorrow can not result from any action or inaction. Similarly, the Bliss or Contentment is never the outcome of fulfillment (of any strong desire) or achievement (of any extraordinary feat). Neither is it the acquisition and possession of things (like finely cut rare diamonds). It is not born of action or inaction. Its Svarupa, Full in Itself, is Nitya mukta, Ananda only; this needs to be understood.

All the Bliss and total absence of Misery is the only intrinsic characteristic of Self Alone (Atma, Brahman). So this perception, this understanding alone, automatically brings about the annihilation of misery/sorrow; it's a natural consequence; 'of' begetting,' 'or 'securing,' 'or 'attaining/achieving.'

It isn't: 'Do something, get rid of this or that –unnecessary things, run away from this, join some Ashram, there you may be relieved of miseries. There is no such promise here. One may go to an Ashram, to the Himalaya, bank of a river, wherever one is; there is no freedom if one carries." this load of misconceptions in one's being. because one has not unburdened 'falsehood' of worldly things; thus, this "a load of sorrow will accompany one wherever one goes.

So, the essence is to "remove" or uproot the misconception and false reality because Atma Reality—Atma Satyatva alone exists, which is Bliss. This misconception must be eradicated, but how do we eradicate it when it is believed to be true? The belief system itself is faulty and defective.

This is akin to a child who is scared of a 'bhuta'—a demon hidden under the bed—which is non-existent and imaginary. Despite the mother's assurances that there is no 'bhuta' at all, the child continues to be gripped by that fear. The 'bhuta' has been imagined out of ignorance; it exists only in the child's mind and is not there in actuality. To dispel this fear, the mother plays a trick: she ties a black thread around the child's arm, claiming it to be a 'shield' against the demon. The child believes in the 'shield' and is freed from fear, and the crying stops. How does this happen? Because of an imaginary 'shield'!

The following day, while giving a bath, the 'shield' slips away from the child's arm and is lost. As night approaches, the child starts feeling scared again because the 'shield' is no longer there to protect him. So, will the bhuta disappear by the mere presence of a black thread? Both the bhuta and the shield are false! This understanding comes through discernment only. The understanding—arivu—is needed here. As long as the scare is in the mind, whether the black thread is there or not, the child is not free of fear.

Similarly, we might say, "Now that I have commenced the spiritual journey, now that I have joined an ashram, etc., I have acquired a considerable amount of discernment, dispassion, etc. The so-called miseries/grief will not bother me, or I am so adequately equipped, and I can grapple with any situation I have control over!" This can lead to over-confidence. Despite sheer hard work and spiritual practices like Japa, Archana, meditation, and Seva, during trying circumstances, individuals may still feel scared and unable to gather enough strength to face challenging situations.

Why is this so? Why do the problems persist? Some may ask, "Why do I face such issues despite being in the Ashrama for a good 30-40 years, doing every kind of spiritual practice with heart and mind?" The answer lies in deep identification with the 'unreal' and self-esteem (abhiman).

Just as the child's fear is not removed by the imaginary shield, spiritual practices alone, without true discernment and understanding of the Self, may not be sufficient to overcome deep-seated fears and misidentifications. The real transformation occurs through true wisdom and realization of the eternal Self, which transcends all false identifications and imagined fears.

4. Beware of Imaginary Advaita

There are no Upanishadic statements that say, "You are not THAT," once you become aware of the Truth, on the basis of the scriptural statements, its job has ended. The truth remains as it is. Through the scriptural statements and the practice of Shravana, Mañana, and Nidhidhyasana (listening, reflection and contemplation), we just become aware of our Self-nature as that Truth.

Normally, what 'IS' is Truth, but what we perceive is Illusion. What exists is a flower garland; what we see is a snake. Now, when we become aware of its reality as a garland, does it change the nature of the garland in any way? No. It remains as it is in the three periods of time i.e. past, present, and future. However, the only change here is in our understanding.

Why do we need this understanding? Because we have become embodied. This is Maya, which is indescribable. How did this happen? Why did the Truth get deluded? No one can explain it. It is beyond explanation (anirvachaniya). However, the delusion (adhyasa) exists due to the lack of enquiry into its nature, but on enquiring into its true nature, our true nature reveals itself.

Again, just because we became aware of our Self-nature, it does not change the nature of the Self in any way. It is simply a knowing, a recognition. So it is important not to expect something extraordinary to happen with this realization, like a great 'bliss' of some sort. All that has happened is recognition of our own true nature as Being-Awareness-Bliss.

It is not like the worshiping of the saligrama stone by imagining the presence of Lord Vishnu in it. There, the saligrama object attains value through our Bhavana (imagination). However, in the case of Self-realization, there is no such added 'gain'. It is simply a recognition of what already is True. There is no further gain or loss. All that has happened is the removal of ignorance through the recognition of Truth.

Where we often go wrong is our additional expectation of the gain of 'Ananda.' It's like feeling the sun being veiled by clouds, or by our thumb. Is that really possible? No. It is only from the standpoint of the observer. The cloud or thumb is insignificant. But the illusion is powerful, and it seemingly covers up the sun. So the necessity of 'understanding' is to simply to see through this ignorance. We need to stop the expectation of additional gain - grand states of bliss. The mind habitually thinks in terms of 'gaining' something. That attitude needs to be dropped. Truth is to simply remove ignorance and the result manifests as awareness of one's Self-nature.

Sat-chit-ananda (Being-Awareness-Bliss) always exists. Why am I not aware of it yet? Due to ignorance. So the necessity here is to remove that ignorance through the recognition of our Self-nature. The Sun has no day or night; it neither rises nor sets; we just impose these states on the sun. Similarly, our true nature neither has the states of waking-dreaming-sleep nor does it have birth or death. We just impose the mind's states of happiness, sadness, etc., on Self-nature. This is a delusion which is beyond description. Thus, we need a firm understanding of our true nature.

Too much expectation of what this state of Self-recognition will bring, in terms of gain, needs to be dropped. Otherwise, it will drag us down. Hence, wisdom is important. Then we will understand our Self-nature correctly. Otherwise, we will be lost in our expectations and keep looking for something in terms of 'gains', a 'goodie bag' of knowledge.

Question- Amma said one does not lose the attitude of being the doer until the state of Jivanmukti is attained.

Response - Doership indeed is avidya, ignorance. Coming to the conclusioDoership is indeed avidya (ignorance). It is like coming to the conclusion that the Sun is easily veiled by placing our thumb in front of our eyes and seeing it as trivial—thus, an illusion loses its importance. From this perspective, the attitude of doership, which stems from the ego, will not last. So, Amma's point is clear.

Question - The attitude of doer-ship, though trivial, does not seem to be easy to get rid of.

Response - That is because we are giving importance to the ego, to this thumb that covers the sun. We need to see it as it is, as trivial, to be free. It is without substance, without reality, if one truly awakens and recognizes one's Self-nature. This understanding of true knowledge becomes the flashlight to dispel the darkness of ignorance.

Question - We have understanding, but we have not yet become a Jivanmukta, hence the trouble.

Response - Do not make Jivanmukti into yet another achievement to be gained by the ego. It is not special, nothing additional to be gained. From the point of Truth, the most important is to understand our own Self-nature. Let us not get confused by overlaying states of Jnana, Jivanmukti, etc. Do not make something out of nothing.

Question - We are giving importance to it because Amma says we have not yet become Jivanmuktas.

Response - what is important is understanding of our Self-nature and not getting lost with self imagined grandeur called jivanmukti. Reflect on the deep sleep, Sushupti. "He, the self-luminous being we are considering, who was identified in the dream state, remains in a state of deep sleep, called

'Samprasāda'—the state of highest serenity. In the waking state, a person accumulates impurities from the many activities of the body and senses; he experiences some relief by discarding them in dreams; but in deep sleep, he achieves the highest serenity (Br Up 4.3.15)" In this waking state, one needs to focus on the state of awareness, the understanding of our true nature. By ignoring the nama-rupa (name-form), we should focus on the underlying substratum of the Self.

They are important to help people enter the path, but once understanding dawns, these things are all inconsequential, and the primary thing becomes the understanding and abiding in our Self-nature. So do not seek special status; just rest in your true nature.

Conclusion

The mind is naturally inclined to seek continuous pleasure. When it shifts from material pursuits to the spiritual path, it does not abandon its quest for pleasure, but instead, seeks that fulfillment from spiritual goals and experiences. Different achievements, insights, and realizations are now sought with the expectation that they will bring continuous happiness and satisfaction. However, this is often a misunderstanding. The truth is that one's inherent nature as Ananda (bliss) is vastly different from the fleeting sensual pleasures associated with worldly experiences. Worldly pleasures, in essence, are merely limited expressions of the infinite consciousness experiencing itself in fragmented forms.

The joy that arises from knowing the truth of one's Self, however, is not transient or subject to the fluctuations of time and circumstances. In a way, this joy is comparable to the state of being physically healthy. When we are healthy, we often take that well-being for granted and are not fully aware of the joy that it brings. However, when we become ill, we yearn for the return of health and feel immense relief and joy when we regain it. Similarly, when one recognizes their true nature as the Self, it brings about a profound sense of well-being, contentment, and inner peace. One feels, "Nothing is wrong with me anymore," and experiences a deep conviction that, "Nothing else needs to be added to this state I am in." This realization is what is known in spiritual terms as mumukshutvam, the intense yearning for freedom from the inherent ignorance of one's true nature, and the desire to return to the state of spiritual wellness.

To experience this spiritual well-being, it is necessary to engage in practices that bring the mind back to its natural state. Repeated practices such as manana (reflection) and nididhyasana (meditation) help the mind to focus on the Self. One of the main obstacles to experiencing the inherent joy of our true nature is the turbulence of the mind, often caused by the dominance of Rajas (restlessness and desire) and Tamas (inertia and ignorance). This turbulence creates a veil that hides the ever-present bliss of the Self. However, knowing one's true Self-nature is not dependent on the mind being still or active—it remains ever-present regardless of the mind's state. Practices that reduce the turbulence of the mind, however, are useful in helping us experience this bliss more directly, even though they are not necessary for the Self to remain as it always is.

It is also crucial to avoid turning jivanmukti (liberation while living) into another goal for the ego to strive toward. The ego often seeks survival by creating future goals, achievements, and milestones to work toward. In the spiritual path, this can manifest as the ego setting its sights on jivanmukti as yet another accomplishment. However, there is a significant difference between the realization of one's true nature as Tattva Jnana (the knowledge of ultimate reality) and continuous abidance in that awareness, which is the state of jivanmukti. Once Tattva Jnana is attained, it is essential to understand that jivanmukti should not be seen as a goal to achieve, but rather as a natural, effortless abidance in one's true nature. Continuous abidance in Awareness, which is the ever-present, true nature of the Self, is both the practice and the goal. When this practice becomes natural and spontaneous, without any effort (sahaja), one attains the state of jivanmukti.

External changes in situations, lifestyles, or practices are often seen as significant in spirituality, but these are ultimately limited. Many people try to leverage spiritual practices or lifestyle changes at the external level, mistakenly believing that these adjustments will lead to divinity or liberation. However, these external adjustments are superficial and have their limitations. True spiritual growth lies in the wisdom of realizing the Self, not in external alterations. Returning to the Self whenever the mind strays is part of the practice, but even this practice has its limitations. The ultimate truth is that we have never left the Self, and we cannot be separated from it. Our true nature is ever-present, ever-conscious, and ever-free. This realization is the essence of Advaita Vedanta, the non-dual understanding that the Self is always whole and complete, regardless of the external circumstances.

True knowledge (jnana) is liberation. It is not an imaginative or projected state created by the mind; rather, it is the direct and immediate realization of the Self as it is. The realization of non-duality, or Advaita, is not something that can be visualized or conceptualized. It is the direct experience of the oneness of existence. In this experience, the individual recognizes that there is no separation between the self and the ultimate reality—there is only One (Ekam), which is the true essence of all beings.

Even if we wish for all beings in the world to be blissful and free from sorrow, we must recognize that such outcomes cannot be achieved through mere wishes or desires. If wishes alone could bring about such changes, the world would already be transformed. Therefore, common sense tells us that we cannot simply will these outcomes into existence. The realization of

Advaita is not an imagined state of oneness (bhavana) or a conceptual understanding of unity. Nor is it the result of any future-oriented goals or achievements. Rather, it is the direct experience of one's true nature (Aparoksha Anubhuti), beyond all mental constructs.

The Chandogya Upanishad discusses Bhuma (the Infinite) as the unchanging reality that is the very nature of Ananda (bliss). This infinite bliss is constant and has no gradations—it is the same in all circumstances and experiences. When we engage in spiritual practices such as chanting Lokah Samastah Sukhino Bhavantu (May all beings everywhere be happy), and participate in seva (selfless service), we must remember to do so without attachment, preferences, or aversions. This is the spirit of "naa dveshti, na kankshati" (neither hatred nor desire). Whatever method or means we choose to engage in, we must always remain clear about the ultimate goal, which is Self-inquiry and the realization of the Self.

Similarly, when we sing hymns such as Mano Buddhi Ahankara Chittani Naaham (I am not the mind, intellect, ego, or memory), we are rejecting these aspects of our experience as "not me." This rejection is not based on personal likes or dislikes, but on the recognition that these aspects of our experience are ultimately unreal. Through the practice of neti neti (not this, not that), we systematically eliminate everything that is not the Self, until what remains is the only truth—the realization of our true nature as pure Awareness.

Should we first accept these unreal aspects as real and then reject them? No, this process is not about accepting the unreal as real but about recognizing that these aspects of our experience are superimposed on the underlying reality of the Self. What is real is Ekam Advitiyam Brahma—One without a second. This should be our understanding.

When we chant Lokah Samastah Sukhino Bhavantu, we must also understand that the intended meaning of the chant is that there is no other reality apart from Ananda Swarupa (the embodiment of bliss). Our chant should not be mechanical or based on an imagined concept of Advaita (bhavana). True Advaita is not based on imagination or wishful thinking. It is the direct experience of oneness that comes from the realization of the Self.

No matter how carefully we try to hide our inadequacies, any pretense or false understanding will eventually be exposed. Therefore, it is essential to remain vigilant, aware, and alert in spiritual practice. We must be careful not to superimpose any aspect of the unreal on the reality of the Self, even in the smallest or most insignificant ways. The Self is inviolate, untouched by the mind, and beyond all superficial characteristics. It is the most subtle, pristine essence of our being.

A devotee, whether a renunciant (sanyasi) or a householder, often perceives the miseries and sorrows of the world as real. In response, they engage in various practices such as seva, japa (repetition of mantras), tapas (austerity), and other spiritual disciplines. They may even shift from one belief system to another, thinking that a different practice or philosophy will provide relief. For instance, someone might turn to Kundalini yoga, believing that it will release them from misery more quickly. However, regardless of how many practices or belief systems they adopt, the outcome remains the same if their mind is still entangled in wrong notions. The solution to worldly miseries does not lie in external practices but in true knowledge (jnana).

In Advaita, or non-duality, there is no "other." The appearance of multiplicity in the world is only valid at the transactional level of reality (vyavaharika), which is temporary and serves practical purposes. At the ultimate level (paramarthika), everything is one. The manifold experiences and forms of the world are merely appearances. They seem to be many, but in truth, they are all expressions of the same underlying reality.

All beings are united in their essence, which is called Svarupa, or the true nature. In the Oneness of existence, which is pure bliss, there is no concept of an "other." Therefore, in this state of unity, there is no distinction between misery and happiness. The Self—whether we call it Atma, Brahman, or by any other name— is Sacchidananda, the embodiment of Existence, Consciousness, and Bliss. It is also Satyam (Truth), Shivam (Auspiciousness), and Sundaram (Beauty). This essence is ever-present, direct, and available to us at all times, independent of any actions we take.

Some people say there are 33 crore deities (devatas), but these too are manifestations of Sat, the ultimate reality. With the right understanding, we should interpret these concepts without attachment or aversion, following the principle of "neither hatred nor desire" (Na dveshti, na kankshati), and come to realize our true Self. We should not promote one viewpoint simply because of personal preference, nor should we reject another for the same reason. We are not saying, "Believe in non-duality" or "Reject duality" based on bias or favoritism.

The real inquiry here is into the nature of Sat—the ultimate reality. This exploration is not driven by emotions but by deep contemplation and mindful awareness.

Imagine going to a jewelry shop where you see different designs with various names and shapes, yet all are made of gold. Similarly, Sat-Chit-Ananda—Existence, Consciousness, and Bliss—is the thread that connects and enlivens everything in the universe. Everything in nature, from plants and animals to the sky, sunrise, and sunset, with all their varying forms and names, is an expression of Consciousness. Just as gold is the unifying substance in all jewelry, Consciousness is the unifying reality behind all existence (Chandogya Upanishad 6.1.5).

By reflecting on these truths, we can begin to live in an awareness of this profound understanding.

So, what can we do to dissolve the illusion of a separate self, to break down the idea of separateness? The key is to recognize the wholeness of existence in the present moment. When we understand this Truth, we naturally embrace the peace and bliss of the Self, which is already whole and complete. This recognition leads to the healing of desires and cravings, and we stop chasing after things like name, fame, or prosperity. The mind, which is constantly looking for fulfillment in the outside world, dissolves when it recognizes the wholeness of the Truth. Conversely, if we try to find fulfillment from the perspective of an incomplete, separate self, our efforts will always fall short.

When we clearly recognize this wholeness, we understand that we already are, where we are, and what we are—the ever-free Self. It's like a wave realizing that it has always been a part of the ocean. We are never separate from the Self; we just need to realize it. When the mind stops its constant activity, the Self—Atma—shines forth naturally.

People seek this stillness of mind in different ways:

- Some use sacred symbols or mantras to quiet the mind.
- Some focus their concentration without the use of imagery.
- Some find peace in nature, outside of any formal belief system.
- Some pursue extreme sports or adventurous activities to still the mind.
- Others find temporary stillness through the enjoyment of food or entertainment.

In all these fleeting moments, people are experiencing glimpses of the wholeness and completeness of Atma, their true nature. However, they often remain unaware of this deeper truth because they are seeking it through temporary and limited means.

Therefore, by recognizing the wholeness of our true nature and dispelling the illusion of separateness, we rest in the absolute bliss that is the essence of our inherent Self.

Self-nature is Bliss

In a deep sleep, we have that experience, as there is only oneness.

From this experience, when we wake up, we say, 'I did not know anything; I slept well.' Because, like the waking state, we did not experience the mind and its varieties, there was only peace and bliss.

But all these are for some time only.

The rest of the time, we are engrossed in thoughts, sensations, perceptions, feelings, sight, sound, touch, etc., which brings disturbances.

Then we go into different moods like anger, desire, jealousy, greed, depression, anxiety, happiness, elation, etc.

When one is constantly faced with these mind tricks, one tries to escape by drugs, etc. Otherwise, go on to a new place to avoid facing the mind directly.

Thus, one feels lost when one cannot succeed in doing so or feels dejected if one gets only a few moments of joy.

In this experimental module, one follows throughout life and dies without knowing the Truth.

So, without being overpowered by the mind and its disturbances, some turn inward to spirituality to recognize Self-nature.

Once one starts to inquire and ask questions regarding that complete bliss, one slowly learns that it is his nature.

Realizing this Truth, one becomes complete in nature.

Conclusion

As expressed in the Chandogya Upanishad 6.1.5:

> yathā somyaikena lohamaṇinā sarvaṃ
> lohamayaṃ vijñātaṃ syādvācārambhaṇam
> vikāro nāmadheyaṃ lohamityeva satyam ||

O Somya, it is like this: By knowing a single lump of
gold, you know all objects made of gold. All changes are
mere words, in name only. But gold is the reality.

This verse beautifully illustrates how understanding the essence
of gold allows one to understand all objects made from gold.
Despite the variety of forms and names, the underlying reality
remains the same—gold.

Similarly, when we focus on the individual names and
forms—ornaments—we overlook the underlying reality of gold.
By failing to recognize this wholeness, our efforts to find peace
become fragmented and limited, leading to more conflicts. We
may compare and classify ornaments as big or small, intricate
or simple, but this only creates complexities instead of seeing
the completeness.

To realize the Truth, we must see the gold, the essence that
is present in all ornaments. The Truth is that the reality of
an ornament is gold, and this same reality is present in every
ornament. Therefore, it is gold that exists at all times. When
we hear this Truth and understand it, all distinctions among
the ornaments are sublated in this understanding. The gold
remains as the fundamental reality, and as gold, all ornaments
are ever free.

In the same way, when we focus on the names and forms of
individuals, deities, and the world, we fail to recognize the Self,
Atma, which is the complete wholeness present at all times.
Without seeing this reality, our efforts to gain peace will be
fragmented and limited, resulting in conflicts.

By comparing and dividing entities like Guru, God, individuals, and the world of names and forms, we introduce complexities instead of understanding the completeness. To realize the
Truth, we must see the Brahman, the Self, which is the reality
of everything. This Truth is always our reality and the reality
of everything.

Therefore, Brahman, the Self, is the only completeness. Hearing this Truth, all individual misconceptions—viewing ourselves as the body-mind-world complex with thoughts, sensations, perceptions, and feelings—are sublated in this understanding. As Satchitananda (Existence, Consciousness, Bliss), we are ever free.

In that completeness, one bows to the lotus feet of the Guru. The Guru blesses the disciple, guiding them towards this realization.

Just as a gold ornament is not separate from the gold and cannot be taken out and kept separately, the 'I' notion in all bodies is the Spurna (effulgence) of the jiva, which is not separate from Brahman. We cannot become separate from the reality of Shiva, the eternal Consciousness. Recognizing this Truth is the essence of realization (Moksha).

Thus, by understanding and realizing the oneness of the Self, we transcend the illusions of individuality and perceive the inherent unity in all existence, attaining peace and liberation.

Why are you not liberated?

The question arises because one feels one is separate from the Self.

What does it mean?

This question will not have arisen if one does not exist as a separate entity. So this means now one thinks one is a separate individual trying to become free because now one doesn't have the freedom in that experience. This creates the idea that maybe someone is free, it may be Guru, and he may help me get that freedom. All these concepts are based on the idea of a separate individual.

So we search for those who have freedom, enlightened Gurus. This is distancing one from freedom instead of becoming free.

It is like trying to separate waves from the water! Waves were never separate from water. Then what is needed here?

Understand that it is modulation of water without changing in a real sense as a wave. It is water alone, seen 'as if' a separate wave.

Similarly, try to separate the individual from Atma, the Self effulgence Consciousness! The individual is never separate from Sat, the Existence. Then what is needed here? Understand that it is a modulation of Consciousness without changing in a real sense as an individual. It is Consciousness alone, seen 'as if' a separate individual.

There may be many waves, but they are not separate from the water. Many bodies may appear and cease as birth and death, but they are not separate from Consciousness.

If it is really separate, we should remove the wave from the water, which is impossible. In Satchitananda, many bodies appear and cease, like in a dream where many-ness, diversity appear and cease.

Who is Swayam Jyothi (Self-effulgence)?

Commonly, one leaves Self-nature by identifying with things that bring all sorts of pleasures or pain. It doesn't matter how small or big the pleasures or pain one is going for because one has already left Self-nature. Those sensations, perceptions, and feelings fake reality when the mind and senses contact the objects. Thus, one completely gets lost in them, trying to enhance them to make them everlasting. It's difficult to realize what one has sacrificed for these pleasures. Thus, it wanders in these until they leave one and bring disappointment or despair. That is why various practices like discernment and dispassion are said and practiced to return to Self-nature.

Through the effulgence of knowingness, its beingness is revealed through and through uninterruptedly as the essence of non-dual. The Self effulgence Consciousness, which is its beingness alone, is revealed all the time exclusively as one wholeness.

When there are no two, then everything is one. It is not Purnam only when one is resting or confined to a certain time, space, or individual. That purnam is not purnam, undifferentiated. So the purnam that was there is now here.

Revealing is indivisible; forsake self-esteem. Based on this Self-nature, understanding what we are, in essence, is what we are using for coming back to the Self. In Self, no samsara means separate from Self; one samsara does not exist that way. Like different from gold, one bangle of gold does not exist that way.

The problems are here only, so we should get the solution here. In a waking state with all empirical activities, the Upanishads say there is no separate reality other than Self-nature. Therefore, all appearances are nothing but an emanation of Sat the Self. So suffering is due to identifying with appearances as reality and saying they trouble 'me.' Here, the Upanishads want us to inquire about the reality nature of 'me' and 'not me.' That means both are nothing but appearances in Consciousness.

In the state of pure Being-Awareness-Bliss (Satchitananda), there is neither grief nor delusion, neither misery nor happiness, nor any of the three states (waking, dreaming, deep sleep), nor can conditions like faintness, Alzheimer's, or coma eclipse it. All spiritual practices aim to realize this Truth. The witness Self (pure awareness) always reveals these states and conditions but remains unchanged. This knowledge liberates one from ignorance, revealing that what truly exists is only Satchitananda.

Swayam Jyothis (the self-luminous one) is making this inquiry, similar to the story of the tenth man. In the story, a group of ten men crosses a river, and upon counting themselves, they repeatedly count only nine, each forgetting to count himself. The one who is counting feels sorrow, thinking the tenth man is lost. When a wise man informs him that he himself is the tenth man, his sorrow vanishes, and he feels happy. However, this happiness is also not his true nature.

His true nature is ever free of sorrow and happiness because he has always been the tenth man, never subjected to any loss. Ignorance made him suffer, but once he realized his true nature, his status did not increase; he merely recognized what was always true. Similarly, his status did not decrease due to his previous ignorance. This illustrates that the true Self is always complete and unaffected by ignorance or knowledge.

'That you are' when told. Do not relate to the dream body-mind-world complex. That's only an appearance. So, gave this knowledge of Sat the Self-nature because one identified with dream body-mind-world complex, which one has nothing to do with. So knowledge removes ignorance; that's it. Hold on to that. Then you are out of the dream.

Sruti says, 'you are that Swayam Jyothi.' Yukthi is the dream. Anubhava is your experience of ever-free Self.

In your room, light is only revealing everything. Hold on to that. Rest What you do is only an interpretation of that light in all your activities.

This awareness is like the light in the room, always present. We often superimpose activities onto the light, saying it illuminates the room, but the reality is that light's intrinsic nature is illumination itself, akin to sunlight.

Similarly, the awareness of 'I' is superimposed on the body-mind-world complex, leading us to say, 'I am seeing, hearing, doing, thinking,' etc. But the reality is that Atma, the Self, has an intrinsic nature of Sat—the beingness, essence, isness, existence—and Chit, the knowingness, consciousness. So, being-knowing is the reality, exclusive and without a second. Thus, recognizing that all activities are just interpretations of this fundamental error superimposed on awareness, we come to the reality of Atma, the Self.

So, when you interact with the world, you interpret the things you perceive based on your mind, thoughts, beliefs, and experiences. All your activities, actions, and thoughts are interpretations of what your awareness reveals to you. By holding to the awareness itself, you gain clarity and stability, recognizing that it is the primary reality. This understanding helps reduce attachment to particular thoughts, emotions, or actions, fostering a more centered and peaceful state of being.

Awareness of Truth

Wave name and form have nothing to do with the water. When we tell a wave, 'you are water,' how can a wave retain its wave nature and realize water nature. Because water nature is free of wave nature, whereas wave nature is impermanent, no reality in itself, they come and go. Arise and cease is its nature. Therefore, if a wave has to let go of its limited nature, then water alone remains. All the while, water alone was.

Instead, if wave doubts the statement 'you are water' saying 'I have a name and form, how can I be limitless water without any name and form? Is that statement true?' If a wave thinks of itself as separate from water, as it has a name and a form, will it make the difference for wave nature to become something other than water?

Whatever a wave may think, it's all water. Water knows this Truth, so it teaches because there is no separateness as a wave. But the wave is not ready to give up and asks the doubts about how is it possible. If so, then why does a wave have a separate name and a form. Then how can a wave rely on the words of water? And so on. Here, the water takes special interest for no reason and starts to explain the wave's real nature. Here, the wave has to listen. Hearing it gets the right understanding. Right understanding brings freedom from limitations. This is how a wave gets completion realizing itself as water ever free of all limitations.

Similarly, individual names and forms have nothing to do with the Self. When we tell aspirants, 'you are that,' how can an individual retain separate nature and realize Self-nature? Because Self nature is free of the body-mind complex nature, whereas individual nature is impermanent—no reality in itself—they come and go. Arise and cease is its nature. Therefore, the individual has to let go of its limited nature; the Self alone remains. All the while, Self alone.

Instead, if an individual doubts the statement 'you are that' saying 'I have a name and form, how can I be a limitless Self without any name or form? Is that statement true?' Suppose an individual thinks of himself as separate from Self as it has a name and a form. Will it make a difference for individual nature to become something other than Self?

Whatever an individual may think, it's all Self. The Self knows this Truth, so it teaches because there is no separateness in a body-mind complex. But the individual is not ready to give up and asks the doubts about how it is possible. If so, then why does an individual have a separate name and a form? Then how can an individual rely on the words of water? And so on. Here, the Self takes special interest for no reason and starts to explain the individual's real nature. Here, the individual has to listen. Hearing it gets the right understanding. Right understanding brings freedom from limitations. This is how a separate self gets completion, realizing itself as Self, ever free of all limitations.

Cessation of Misunderstanding

Each dream is separate. No one can share the dream with others. It applies to all. You are all the characters in my dream, and 'I am' the lead role. Misunderstanding 'me' in a dream is the problem of 'dream me' with 'dream you,' and the peace with 'me' is no more problem to 'dream me' with 'dream you.' Even though 'I' created a dream, 'I' don't have any responsibility for ongoing good, bad, or ugly activities. 'I am' untouchable, unreachable, Self effulgence Consciousness.

Sleep is the cause of the dream. Similarly, ignorance is the cause of the present long dream. So waking is a dream only. But long. Once one wakes up, the ignorance ends.

One who overcomes ignorance ends the dream. When awakening, no more dreams, and all their characters. All end. There is no bondage or liberation, as everything is one jiva reflection. No one is liberated, as it is my dream. The moment 'I' wake up, everything ends. All the while, one is Self illumining Consciousness. But because of his ignorance, he himself, with all his characters, appears.

'I' created all these characters, 'me' and 'not me.' So interactions, actions, and reactions do not influence the creator, 'I.' It is like the ongoing movie does not influence the screen. All are appearances on screen. Once it ends, only the screen remains.

No one is liberated, as 'I am' the one who is there. With this knowledge, the dream is over. Only self-effulgence (Swayam Jyothi) is there. Everything is the appearance of Swayam Jyothi.

With this Awareness of Self, when we do all our day-to-day transactions, spiritual or worldly activities will not create the illusion of a separate self.

5. The Guru's Guidance

"Living with Mother is like being in an airplane as it moves on its way to the take-off point. First the airplane moves slowly out of the airdrome towards the runway; it then moves faster and faster along the runway until it finally takes off. If one learns to live in Mother's presence with an attitude of love and self-surrender, it will certainly bring one to the take-off point. In Mother's presence you do not remain the same—you are constantly changing internally. The old patterns disappear as you move deeper and deeper into the new realms of your true existence."

-Amma

All of us have decided to walk the spiritual path. You could say that it is due to God's grace or Guru's grace. We have come to understand that there is really no true happiness in this world. However great our achievements in this world may be, we understand that one does not find fulfillment in this world. But walking on the spiritual path does not mean coming to or living in an ashram. It is really about the spiritual inquiry within.

Our focus should really be on our true nature- 'Who am I?'. One can be a young student, a householder doing her daily job, a sanyasi in an ashram, or a person leading a retired life. The stage of life or kind of job one is engaged in matters little. The essential thing, though, is to adjust our life situation so that it does not interfere with our spiritual progress.

Spirituality is not about trying to live a poor life, or doing things like eating just rice gruel, sleeping on the floor, eating sparingly, or wearing a certain type or color of clothes, etc. It is not just about practicing austerities or living a simple lifestyle. In the olden days, spiritual aspirants used to go to the forest or beg for food in villages. However, those practices should not be our focus in the present times.

Spiritual aspirants today are very much in touch with society, whether we live in an ashram or at home. Changing one's location has not changed the link with society. There is really no need to give up our jobs or other worldly responsibilities. Where we stay, what we eat, what we wear and so on is not an obstruction to our spiritual life, as long as we focus on our real internal nature, rather than on external aspects of life.

We need to earn an income to maintain a family or to practice charity, like supporting an ashram through donations. So earning income through honest, truthful means is not wrong. Eating poorly, fasting, avoiding sleep, or other physical hardships are not spirituality. Neither does eating healthy food with adequate amounts of protein and so on go against spirituality.

On the spiritual path, we reflect on who or what God or reality is. Before embarking on our spiritual path, we had a mental concept of what God was. Each religion has its own practices, rituals, and beliefs. But the deep thinkers or spiritual philosophers, such as Shankara, Plato, or great Christian or Sufi saints, these great souls have found out the Truth and experienced God face-to-face. They have shared these Truths with us in the form of the Mahavakyas such as 'You are That reality' (Tat twam asi). They point out that the focus should be on our real nature. They remind us that our real nature is Sat-Chit-Ananda (Being-Awareness-Bliss), that freedom (Mukti) is our real nature.

We normally think of ourselves as individuals with a body, mind, thoughts, feelings, emotions, etc. That is how we live our day-to-day life, sometimes getting angry, sometimes being impatient, sometimes being happy, sometimes being unhappy, sometimes losing our balance, but other times exhibiting good behavior. Even though sometimes we feel that we are in a win-win situation despite thinking of ourselves as individuals, at other times we experience negative states of mind and life situations that are painful.

In order to help us avoid such ups and downs, the Guru inculcates in us qualities such love, compassion and a service (seva) mindset. Through such practices, we start to attain a certain degree of evenness, purity of mind (chitta shuddhi) and attain one pointedness of mind. Guru then points out that we need to move further from our external focus to an internal focus.

Mental purity (chitta shuddi) by itself is not enough to know the Truth. Our spiritual practices help us to know the Truth but they are not the Truth. We might spend all our time in spiritual practices like Japa, Sevas, Bhajans, Pujas, spiritual talks, etc., but they are not an end in themselves. Our spiritual practices must ultimately help us realize our True nature. In general, external practices are like keeping a spring compressed with our fingers. Ultimately, we remove our hand when it begins to hurt. Similarly, practices are not the end in themselves. We might feel we have a certain degree of control over our minds through such practices, but if we ease up on the practices, the mind will return to its old patterns. So, while we continue to perform our spiritual practices, we should also start focusing on understanding who we really are, our essential nature.

So these practices help us gain clarity of the mind, but we have to take the next step after achieving this one-pointedness of the mind. This next step is to inquire into the Truth and understand what our real nature is. This is the focus of the Upanishads. Their focus is on our real nature. The real nature of the inquirer, the spiritual seeker, we have forgotten our real nature and got drowned in the ocean of worldliness (samsara). In the story of the tenth man, the tenth man felt sad because he believed one in the group was lost, since he could only count nine others in the group. When the tenth man is told that he himself is the tenth man, he is able to drop his sadness. Similarly, the Upanishad says that we are that Brahman or the universal Self. We are what we have been looking for all this time.

It is really having the conviction that we are really Brahman. Being always the Universal Self, we forget our real nature and think of ourselves as individuals. The Upanishads remind us that our real nature is the Universal Self. The aim of the Guru is to convey to us the truth about our real nature.

In most traditions, spiritual practices often adopt a certain attitude to assist in worship (Upasana). For example, in the Hindu tradition, a Saligram stone (smooth stone from the Gandaki river) is treated as a symbol of Vishnu and people worship it. Even though it is only a smooth stone, we view it as a symbol of Vishnu and perform Upasana. Similarly, If we grew up as Hindus, we would view God as Vishnu, Shiva, Kali, Ganapathi, etc. We pray to them, converse with them and make promises to them. All these practices help us to purify and gain clarity of mind.

Similarly, many feel that the good things in life are due to the grace of God (Ishwara) or Guru. Millions of people visit temples like Tirupathi or Palani because they get peace and fulfillment from visiting these spiritual places. It is their faith in these spiritual places that gives them peace. What is really happening is that such visits help us to still the mind, and the Self is reflected in that stillness.

In our relationship with the Guru, it is similar. We adopt a certain attitude, see the Guru as a symbol of God, and perform puja for the Guru. We see all the Gods embodied in the Guru. We do Guru pada seva, serve the Guru and in every way, see the Guru as God. All these are helpful in creating mental purity and one-pointedness of mind. When Amma hugs us or when Amma looks at us, in that instant, our mind becomes still and we feel fulfilled. We pray to God or the Guru intensely through bhavana (by strongly feeling that Guru is a symbol of God), we achieve these benefits, which remain in our minds for a short duration.

After gaining this one-pointedness of mind, we need to take the next step of finding out, 'What is my real nature? Who am I?'

How should I find out my real nature? How can I gain a firm conviction about the Truth? First, I have to understand that my current problems exist because of an incorrect understanding of Self, and that I have a real nature beyond this individual nature. The Guru tells us that our real nature is Atman or Brahman. When the disciple asks the Guru, 'please teach me the Truth,' the Guru tells us that our real nature is That pure reality and that we are never different from that Brahman at any time. The Guru here is speaking about the nature of the disciple (the one who is asking the question and listening to the Guru), who is Brahman himself.

Our Upanishads say that when the disciple asks the Guru, or similarly when Maitreyi asks her sage husband Yagnavalkya, or when Svethaketu asks his father Uddalaka, or when Nachiketa asks Yama the God of death, these great spiritual gurus are really conveying our real nature to us (the nature of the one who is asking). The Amrita Tatvam (the Truth that makes us immortal) is being explained to us by these great teachers. The Guru has great wisdom about our real nature. When we ask such mahatmas, please teach me so that I can also be in the same blissful state (ananda swarupam) as you, They convey the Truth to us so that we may become free from our perceived bondage.

Most of us see the Guru as God and keep the Guru in great reverence. Just like we respect a PM or a President, we normally view the Guru as an individual and offer our deep respect. Just as we think of ourselves as a person, we think of the Guru as a person. The difference between the Guru and the ordinary person is that the Guru has knowledge of the Self. The true nature of both the Guru and the disciple is the same. We should see the Guru as the one who can convey the Truth about our real nature and approach such a mahatma and ask her - 'Please teach me and help me gain that status that you are in so that I also can be in that state of Ananda'. Then, through compassion without any reason, the Guru tells the disciple how he/she can attain the same status by becoming aware of their true nature.

Let us take the example when Vivekananada asks Sri Ramakrishna about his spiritual experience. When Vivekananda questions Sri Ramakrishna whether his experience of the Truth is just specific to him or if it was attainable by anyone else. Sri Ramakrishna immediately answers, saying that anyone can attain his state and asks Vivekananda if he wants to get that experience. So the main interest of the Guru is to convey the Truth that she has experienced to the disciple through teaching by word of mouth. So we really have to focus on the message that the guru is conveying. We have to see the Guru as the Truth she is conveying and not as an individual. We normally see the guru as an individual with a human body and mind and thus limit the guru. Here, the Guru is not a person but the Truth that she is conveying to the disciple about the real nature of the disciple. Our focus should be on the message that the Guru is conveying.

Our focus should be on Guru's words that tell us that our real nature is ever-present, ever-pure, ever-aware, and ever free (Nitya, Suddha Buddha Mukta). Through the guru's instruction (upadesam), we need to understand that our real nature is that unchangeable reality. Our focus has to shift from Guru's physical form to the message conveyed by the guru that we are Sat-Chit-Ananda (Being-Awareness-Bliss). That is why Sri Shankara says 'Guru naiva Shisya' - neither Guru nor Disciple. The meaning here is that we should focus on the Truth taught by the Guru and not on viewing the Guru and disciple as individuals.

We notice that Amma addresses us by first saluting us as embodiments of love (prema swarupa), embodiments of Brahman (atma swarupa). Amma sees us as atman and not as individuals, and she uses every opportunity to remind us of our essential nature. That Atma, which is ever Pure and Free (Nitya suddha Mukta) is you. Guru converts the Upanishad into a vocal instruction. Ultimately through God's grace (Iswara krupa, Guru krupa), we will understand that everything around us is God. So with God's grace, Guru's grace, and our own Atma's grace, we have to inquire into our real nature.

Amma's Example of Living as Awareness

One day, I was sitting with Amma and found that she exemplifies a profound commitment to her followers, a dedication that transcends her personal well-being. Amma was saying to the Swamis sitting in her room, "Despite not feeling well, I practice 'Neti, Neti'—'not this, not that', a method often used to understand the Self by discerning what it is not. I use it to move beyond my physical ailments and come out to meet people."

Amma added that she makes a conscious decision to attend meditation, bhajan, and darshan, driven by the thought of her children who come to see her. She acknowledges that many of them might have significant problems or urgent issues to share, understanding that some might not have another chance to meet her due to the uncertainties of life. This deep sense of responsibility and compassion for her followers compels her to push through her own discomfort. Preparing herself to meet her children, Amma overcomes feelings of laziness and lethargy. Amma says that once she arrives in the hall and sits among her children, any sense of unease dissipates. In their presence, she finds her energy renewed and her inner health lifted. This act of self-negation, of putting the needs of her followers above her own, is a testament to her unwavering devotion and love. It's a powerful reminder of the strength that can be found in selflessness and the transformative power of compassion and empathy.

Her approach to dealing with her followers is deeply transformative. For Amma, the mere act of being present with her children—listening to their troubles, sharing in their joys and sorrows—becomes a healing process. It showcases how empathy and caring for others can dissolve personal barriers of discomfort and fatigue. This reciprocal flow of love and understanding highlights the oneness of human experiences. Furthermore, Amma's actions demonstrate the strength that lies in vulnerability and openness. By acknowledging her own struggles yet choosing to rise above them, she sends a powerful message about the human capacity to overcome challenges through the strength of the heart. Her example inspires resilience and courage in the face of adversity. The impact of Amma's selflessness extends beyond the immediate moments of interaction. It creates ripples in the lives of those she touches, encouraging them to embody similar qualities in their own lives. As they carry these experiences with them, the seeds of compassion and empathy are sown in broader communities, fostering a more caring and understanding world. Amma's life is a testament to the transformative power of selflessness. Her dedication serves as a beacon, guiding us toward the understanding that true strength is found in the ability to give of oneself selflessly, to empathize with others, and to meet the world with an open heart. This lesson is not just a philosophical concept, but a practical guide for 'Living As Awareness,' a life filled with compassion and empathy.

Amma's Wisdom

> *"Love is in the present, happiness is in the present, God is in the present and enlightenment is also in the present"*
> - Amma

Amma's profound statement encapsulates the essence of non-duality, emphasizing that love, happiness, God, and enlightenment are all rooted in the present moment. This wisdom invites us to recognize the inherent unity that underlies these

aspects of existence, highlighting the profound interconnectedness of all things.

Awareness about the Self begins with the guidance of Sruti
Matha, who, in Amma's teachings, represents the Divine Mother
and the source of wisdom. It is through her divine grace that
the ancient Vedic aphorism "Tat twam asi" (Thou art That) is
brought into the present moment. This timeless wisdom, when
placed in the context of the present, serves as a transformative
catalyst.

Upon hearing or reading these words, one becomes aware
of the nature of the Self, transcending the limitations of the
egoic self. Just as a room's light becomes apparent when we
are made aware of its ever-present existence, the true nature
of the Self dawns upon us when we realize that it is eternally
present in the now.

Enlightenment, in this context, is not a distant goal to be
achieved but a state of awareness that arises when we recognize
the immediate and ever-present nature of our true Self. The
process is akin to becoming aware of the light in the room—it
was always there, but our awareness of it was veiled until it
was brought to our attention. Similarly, the Self, as Brahman,
has always been our absolute nature, but our awareness of it
was obscured by the complex interplay of the body, mind, and
external world.

When we are told about the Self as our ultimate reality, the
illusion of the body-mind-world complex begins to dissolve. This
complex, which seemed so real, is negated and sublated in the
light of this awareness. What remains untouched and eternal
is the Self, our absolute nature.

Enlightenment, in its truest sense, is the direct realization
that the individual self and the universal Self are one and the
same. Just as recognizing the presence of light in the room
dispels darkness, understanding the Self as Brahman dispels
the illusion of separateness and reveals the ultimate truth. This

realization is the essence of Amma's teaching and the core of non-dual wisdom.

In conclusion, Amma's teaching beautifully illustrates the non-dual understanding that love, happiness, God, and enlightenment are all intrinsic to the present moment. The recognition of the Self as Brahman, as guided by Sruti Matha, leads to the profound realization that we are, and always have been, in the presence of our true nature. This awareness is the ultimate enlightenment, transcending the illusions of the egoic self and revealing the unity of all existence.

6. Poems and Reflections

Know What You Already Are

What you are is the simplest and most direct proof of your Self,
It cannot disappear, be changed, altered, separated, modified, or destroyed,
The moment you search for the divine or sacred,
you move away from what you are,
What you are stops everything you look for.

In fact, you are looking for what you are in everything,
What you are is not an image, a name, or a product of the mind-body complex,
It is free of all identifications and is the perfume of everything,
What you are is inseparable from all activities – seeing, hearing, and so on.

Whatever that is by which all sensations, perceptions, and feelings are known is what you are,
Its beauty is seen in everything, and its presence is felt in everything,
It is intrinsic in all modulations of thought, and all actions are its expressions,

The whole movement is the proof of what you are, ever free.
What you are is the very inherent nature of oneself and everything,

It is unblemished, free of conflicts, pure awareness, and
ever-free in nature,
What you are is independent and does not need any help,
In fact, it helps everything by breathing its very nature into
all.

All scriptures point to what you are, but what you are does
not need any pointers, as it is its own proof,
Nothing divine or sacred is separate from what you are,
What you are is the whole truth by its very nature,
Knowing what you are is the key to understanding the Truth
of Existence.

Reflections on Dying

One often wonders what happens during death? And what
happens to one after they die?
Death marks the conclusion of an organism's journey from
birth,
But does life truly cease with the body's failure?
Amma says, Like a blown fuse in a light bulb, does electricity
vanish?
Or do we simply replace the bulb, allowing the current to
flow once more?
In the human body, when the physical form expires like a
blown fuse,
A new bulb replaces it, while the current remains unaffected.
Thus, Amma says beauty endures while the flower withers,
Similarly, exclusive Beingness persists while the physical
body falls.

What is freedom?

Understanding Self's nature, free of birth and death, is
freedom's essence.
Bound by society's beliefs and concepts, we remain ensnared,

Illusions we cherish, unaware of Truth's clarity, like a dream.
From childhood, life's concept we've embraced, rooted in falsehood,
Yet fail to ponder life's deeper truths as the curtain falls.
We pass on these illusions to our children, perpetuating the cycle,
Lost in false concepts, facing death's approach with confusion.

Death, a phenomenon of beauty, untaught by society's institutions,
When sickness strikes, we seek treatment, yet death's approach met with fear.
Embrace its arrival with courage, for death is not the end,
Resistance only amplifies suffering, acceptance brings peace.

Death is not unknown, but the conclusion of life's journey,
Immortality resides in the Self, existing beyond time's constraints.
Creation, sustenance, destruction, an eternal cycle,
A process spanning millennia, beyond human comprehension.

Life and death, a play of Consciousness, waves in the ocean,
A magician's show, where the end signals a new beginning.
Relationships, fleeting scenes in life's grand theater,
As one act ends, another begins, in an eternal cycle.

All occurrences unfold within Consciousness,
In deep sleep, we abide as Consciousness alone.
In waking, life's unfolding drama, like a map unfurled,
Life and death, like a pendulum's swing, ceasing with time's passage.

Consciousness, the ultimate reality, where all begins and ends,
Infinite, immortal, pure, ever-present, the essence of Self.
You are THAT, the eternal Self, beyond the grasp of death's embrace.
In Consciousness, there is no death, only eternal existence.

Be Free, O Sadhu!

O Sadhu, nothing in the world is everlasting,
Attractions and repulsions are bound to happen,
They are but the nature of the body-mind-world complex,
Yet, they are not yours! O Sadhu, You are the Immutable, ever-free Self.

Nobody can tell you what to do,
Who can lead or bind you? O free one,
Share the pointers of the Truth with all,
O Sadhu, remind them of their boundless nature.

All manifested objects depend on you for support,
Yet you are completely free of all,
Never consider yourself to be one who is born or to be bound,
Remember you are unconditioned and Ever-free,
O Sadhu, rest as That.

Never accept the weakness of the body-mind complex,
Never relate to others as an individual,
Who can exert their authority on you? O free one,
All such doctrines are for the weak,
O Sadhu, you are the eternal one.

Attractions can come to you,
But you know they are all impermanent,
There is nothing that can trick your understanding,
O Sadhu, All attractions are trivial.

Treat all phenomena as nothing, like an illusion,
See the plight of those,
Who are carried away by the winds of desires,
O Sadhu, Lost in that search, never to return.

From all the confusions of the world,
Say you are done with them,
No one and nothing can touch you,
O Sadhu, You are That Untouchable Truth.

Do not ask 'What should I do?'
You are ever the non-doer and non-enjoyer,
Accept or reject not, respond spontaneously when needed,
Otherwise, rest as Awareness, as YourSelf, O Sadhu.

Dance with nature, sing with nature, fly with the birds,
Feel the lightness in your heart,
Enjoy God's creation to the fullest,
O Sadhu, Until it is time to offer the body-mind complex back
at the altar of Death.

Enlighten the ones who seek thy refuge with the Truth,
Well, it's all a staged play, to come back to the Truth,
We are not meant to cling, only to witness,
O Sadhu, Thus help set them free.
All fail to reflect,
Because they feel they can rule the world,
Seeing the futility of their ego,
O Sadhu, Remind them to seek within.

Unconditional Freedom

When Sruti reveals that our nature is Brahman, the entirety,
The aspirant, upon hearing these words, gains understanding.

Within the Self, Samsara is nonexistent; thus, all superimposed miseries are extinguished.
The insight reveals that our intrinsic nature is indeed that of wholeness.

Following this realization, all actions are undertaken with this newfound understanding,
Never again entangling with Samsara or harboring the sentiment of belonging to it.
With every misunderstanding dispelled, the "I" remains perpetually liberated from Samsara.
This profound truth is then shared with others, guiding them towards this enlightening knowledge.

Light remains untouched by the instruments through which it shines;
Its essential nature is to emanate brilliance.
In a similar vein, the Self transcends the body-mind-world complex,
Wherein one's identity as "I" dissolves;
understanding that the "Self is Brahman" heralds Truth

Finding Light and Freedom

We don't know where we're going,
Nor do we know where we're from.
Even now, we're unsure of our purpose,
So we keep living in uncertainty.

We all just want to be comfortable,
But we're clueless on how to achieve it.
Is crying till we die all we're going to do?
Can we ever find peace in this life?

Then, in the darkest times, a light appears,
Guiding us, showing us the way.
This light, a guru, tells us we're actually free,

Helping us see the Truth.

Recognizing this Truth, one cries tears of joy,
I was never bound, never born,
Nowhere have I come from, and nowhere to go,
I am peace itself, the search has ended.

Realizing the Eternal Presence

"Realize this light," Amma instructs us,
"Follow what Sruti teaches you."
We're on a quest to discover who we truly are,
And we learn, just as they said, we are complete and whole.

With this realization, our hearts find tranquility,
Understanding, we are always That.
Every step, every breath, becomes lighter,
We align with the Truth, the Sruti way.

No longer ensnared by worries or fears,
With this knowledge, we realize we are presence.
We recognize our True nature, ever free,
Brahman itself, without a second, forever.

7. Love Letters to a Monk

Questions from a young aspirant

Question 1

Swamiji, I have a fundamental question to ask. Why is it said that nothing in the world can satisfy us eternally? Is it because the object of pleasure is not permanent? But isn't pleasure itself something that can be made permanent by pursuing and accumulating different objects that provide pleasure? So why can we not make this enjoyment, this pleasure last? What is wrong with an object which we derive pleasure from?

Or is this the wrong line of questioning? If we follow this thought process, we'll be in deep, deep trouble, I guess?

Reply

It is important to reflect on a few things before we probe this question. First of all, it is essential that we do not hesitate to inquire into anything that is a source of conflict within. If we do not, then it becomes a potential stumbling block for us in the future. When emotions are triggered by desire, the conflicts become even harder to deal with. A clear understanding and wisdom are our best defenses, enabling us to step back from mental activity when desires and other emotions arise in relation to objects of temptation.

Secondly, remember that in Sanatana Dharma, liberation is not the only goal of human life. Dharma (right action driven by the right attitude), Artha (prosperity), Kama (fulfillment of desires), and Moksha (liberation) are described as the four goals of life. With a foundation rooted in the wisdom of Dharma, humans are encouraged to pursue prosperity along with the fulfillment of their desires. In pursuing these things, do so with wisdom so that neither you get hurt, nor would you need to hurt others to achieve those things. The final is Moksha, which completes our life—this process or journey to end this life without any regrets or remorse. This Self-realization is the goal. This peace is complete in understanding that oneself is not just a body-mind complex born to die. In fact, your essential nature is ever-free, peace, bliss, and fulfillment are your ever-present nature.

With this being said, let us investigate the question of what is wrong with seeking objects of pleasure, and why is it said that these objects cannot satisfy us eternally.

Eternally is a big word. When it comes to every single object in nature, you know that nothing that arises or is born can remain permanent. Generally, people are afraid to accept this fact. We are confused and search for permanence, but we fail because the nature of all objects themselves is subject to change. When this understanding becomes established in us, acceptance starts. We know that the nature of fire is to give heat, light, and splendor. Then we do not seek to change it. Instead, we use it according to its nature. Such is the state of all objects, including our body and mind. Use everything according to its nature. Then we do not get burned by fire. Likewise, we do not get dejected when something arises and ceases. When we understand that pain and pleasure, birth, and death are similar, this understanding brings wisdom.

Our experiences in life have shown that, despite our best efforts, we have failed to attain and hold onto lasting pleasure. Even though we know it is impossible, we still strive to make it permanent. Patanjali's Yoga Sutra 2:15 is a good one to reflect on here - It says:

pariṇāma tāpa saṁskāra duḥkhaiḥ guṇa-vṛtti-
virodhācca duḥkham-eva sarvaṁ vivekinaḥ

'To the discriminative one, everything is laced with
suffering, because all things are of the nature of being
ever changing, difficult to attain and hold on to, and
because the nature (gunas) of the object is often at
odds with the state of one's body and mind'.

What it means is, all things are painful because of the effort
involved in obtaining an object of pleasure, holding onto it,
making sure it continues to give me pleasure, and also ensuring
I am in the right state of body-mind to enjoy that pleasure. All
of this is HARD work. This is why in the Gita Ch 5:22, Sri Krishna
calls sense pleasures Dukha-yonaya - that is, a womb of sorrow.

It is undeniable that when hungry, a good meal is wonderful,
and nature is wonderful, for example: sunset, mountains, etc.
The problem is the effort involved in obtaining all these pleasures. If one neither craves, nor dislikes what life brings in our
path, then we will be fine.

Lastly, it is important to remember that there is really no
'object out there'. It is all within. All experiences happen in one's
own mind. Whatever sensations or experiences we perceive,
it is just a thought; it arises and ceases, as is the nature of all
thoughts, feelings and emotions. That is why we have had a
variety of experiences. Otherwise, one homogeneous experience should have been there, but homogeneity is not one's
experience. If such continuous pleasure was indeed what we
sought, why do all beings drop everything and go to sleep? In
sleep, all experiences are dropped, and yet we feel good when
we wake up. It is not that we always have to hold on to some
experiences at the physical or mental levels to get satisfaction.
We obviously see that even when no experiences are there in
sleep, we are at peace, It is rejuvenating. Eternal satisfaction is
just a misnomer. Be in the present. The present moment is the

only truth. Then we are ever at peace. We need not crave it. It is there for us. Welcome to it, and you are home.

The Self is the one that gives Reality to the body-mind-world complex, like water, which gives reality to the wave. Each 'object out there' is just a modulation of Existence, Awareness, and bliss. That's the Truth. This right knowledge frees the false impressions and beliefs about objects like the body-mind-world complex.

Question 2

I struggle with relationships. When I reflect on it, I get that what we are really seeking is 'ego pampering'. Theoretically, I understand that this psychological entity that I take myself to be, is seeking out other such entities that are compatible in order to share knowledge, seek appreciation, physical pleasure, psychological validation and so on. I also understand that by doing so, by seeking these relationships, I might be strengthening my identification with the body-mind complex. What I do not understand though is the why?

It is the experience of everyone that this dependence on another being makes us terribly suffer or dependent. When relationships break apart, they cause tremendous pain and inner conflict, leaving behind deep scars. We enjoy the company of like-minded people, but often we find that there is no reciprocation of our love and affection. We suffer because we are dependent on them, yet we are not finding what we seek. Our identities are shaped by our success or failure in relationships, and past failures create a sort of victim mindset in us, and what's worse is that we then approach other activities with this mindset, making things even worse.

Despite all this, we continue to try to make relationships work. Why this madness? Is it just because humans are social beings and it is bound to be so, or is there something else going on?

Reply

All relationships are pursued for the sake of one's own Self. Everyone loves one's 'Self' the most. Due to our lack of understanding of the true nature of our 'Self', we seek out relationships with the erroneous belief that these relationships will provide us a feeling of fulfillment, a feeling of expansiveness of self. One may think that they love others, but what one really loves is what they 'get' from that relationship. In the Brihadaranyaka Upanishad 2.4.5, Yajñavalkya explains this same concept to his wife Maitreyi -

> "It is not for the sake of the beings, my dear, that they are loved, but for one's own sake that they are loved. It is not for the sake of all, my dear, that all is loved, but for one's own sake that it is loved. The Self, my dear Maitreyī, should be realized. It should be heard of, reflected on and meditated upon."

Since most people are ignorant of the essential nature of one's own Being, they feel a lack, loneliness, or boredom they want to fulfill. They feel that maybe by seeking someone or something, they would get joy and fulfillment. Thus, we see the mad rush in the world where people are seeking to expand their sense of 'I' and 'mine' through accumulation. They seek out relationships, wealth, power, influence, experiences, and anything else that they believe will give them what they seek. "Anything that increases this sense of 'I' and 'mine'" is their strategy. Needless to say, we see that this has never worked for anyone.

Do you know the story of Mulla Nasruddin and his search for the missing key?

One day, people saw Mullah Nasruddin out in the street searching frantically for something.

"What are you searching for, Mullah? They enquired.

"I've lost my key," replied Mullah.

People tried to help him, so they joined him in the search. Some time passed and the key was still not found. So someone asked him "Where exactly did you lose the key? Do you remember?"

"I lost the key in the house," replied the Mulla.

"Then why are you searching for it in the street?!" asked the people.

"Because there is more light here." Replied the Mulla

This short story is symbolic. Everybody is looking for the key to happiness, but they are looking for it in the wrong place. It is not to be found outside.

All such seeking makes our identification with the ego stronger. Due to our incorrect self-understanding, we believe the body, mind and the world filled with objects to be real, and seek to pursue objects, people and experiences that bring pleasure and avoid those that do not. Until this incorrect understanding is corrected, there is no chance for one to find any peace or satisfaction.

We need to investigate who we really are. Who is this entity that says 'I'? We believe ourselves to be many things. We associate all sorts of labels with ourselves, based on our gender, country of origin, job title, education, and so on - but when we seek what is behind all of these labels, what we find is That which is changeless. We must pursue this line of inquiry in light of the teachings of our Guru and the Upanishads. They point out 'you are That'. When they say 'That', what is being pointed to is Brahman, which is the very essence of all existence. Your essential nature is that of fullness, of absolute consciousness, peace and bliss. Due to the fact that we are unaware of this Truth, believing ourselves to be limited and incomplete, we seek people and objects in the hope that they provide us with fulfillment, a sense of expansiveness, security and validation for our identity. Seeing this very clearly brings one out of this self-ignorance.

One is ever free, not bound. This realization is freedom from ego. When one sees the fact, the psychological entity is dropped along with all doubts and contrary thinking that results from believing oneself to be the body-mind complex. This clarity comes from hearing and reflecting on One's True Nature. This brings the right understanding regarding one's true nature.

You say the past relationships have left scars, which now further influence your daily interactions with others. Do you see how much faith you are placing in what you take yourself to be? This ego personality that gets hurt, or grows proud and so on is unreal, but you have invested much in it. Now, anything anyone does or says that does not acknowledge your made-up ego identity hurts you. How can this self-created pain be fixed by anything external - when this whole structure is fictional? We can hardly see the Truth when our minds are busy with the imagined thoughts, feelings and emotions. Meanwhile, we believe that the source of all this is external, that someone or something 'out there' is the cause of all our problems. We need to see this fact clearly, and not get hurt when something doesn't work out the way the ego wants.

I am not saying to avoid all people and relationships, but we need to understand relationships for what they are. They are not a place to seek happiness and fulfillment. Remember what Amma says -

"If we live with the right understanding of the nature of the world, then whatever our situation may be in life, and whatever experiences come our way, we will be prepared to face them and accept them with mental equipoise.

When we understand the nature of the world, we won't get unnecessarily upset when a disappointment comes our way; we will have anticipated it, and thus be mentally prepared to cope with it.

What is the nature of the world? It is always selfish. People value a cow and keep it only because of its milk. The day the cow stops giving milk, the owner won't hesitate to sell it to the butcher. As long as we rely on the world for our support, we will continue to experience sorrow and suffering, because that support will not always be there."

It is important for us to internalize what Amma is teaching here. Most relationships or friendships start out fine because there is still the expectation that what one is seeking might be found through the other individual. However, most relationships or friendships soon fail because both of the individuals in the relationship are seeking from each other. They are there to get what they want, and not give. This soon creates stresses and strains, finally leading to misery and hurt.

As long as we think, 'I am here and the world is out there', this feeling of separation brings fear and a lack of completeness or fulfillment. Because of this, we seek to overcome this feeling of separation. Until one is ignorant about reality, which is 'One, whole, undivided Truth', we continue to engage in division and relationships. This fragmented thinking is mind-created, ego-created, or false self-creation, which is the cause for all wars within and outside the world.

According to Upanishadic wisdom, this division can only be rectified by the realization of Oneself.

The rishis point out, 'Self alone is the Truth, and it is fearless in nature as it knows nothing that is apart from itself.' This perceived world has no reality apart from the Self. When we free ourselves from ignorance regarding this Truth, by seeking the wisdom of the Guru and the Upanishads, we realize that our true nature is free of all identities, free from the concepts of time and space, independent of the three states of waking, dreaming and sleep, like that of a crystal, which merely reflects the color of the objects placed near it. Lack of this Self-knowledge is like darkness, so bring the light, which is the right knowledge about Oneself, where all the ghost-like ignorance gets negated. Rest in your essential nature as this Self, which is One, nondual, existence, Consciousness, bliss, Ever Free, Birthless and immortal.

Question 3

I often experience terrible inner turbulence, most often it is due to relationships. It sometimes feels unbearable. How do I deal with situations such as this?

Reply

Whether the relationship works out or fails, you are in trouble both ways. You are perpetuating an individuality either way. This individuality that you try to perpetuate is not real. It is unreal, like a mirage, like a sky flower that does not exist. Both individuals in the relationship are usually trying to cling to a made-up false self image that has no independent existence. This mad clinging on to this imaginary self is the cause of Samsara, which does not allow us to see our true nature. This mad clinging is like being a larva or a cocoon. The worm eats up the leaves to make a shell and lives inside that shell. The only freedom for that larva is death when the weaver kills it and uses it to make silk clothes. Likewise, we are doomed when we cling to individuals, hoping that this particular relationship will save us. We are trying to embrace a crocodile and believe that it will save us. All concepts about oneself, which one has cherished since childhood, have bound one like the silkworm with its cocoon. We have been living this life of lies throughout our lives, searching for permanent happiness outside.

In one of Amma's Bhajans, it says, "Jeevita Veedhiyil Mullum Poovum," Life may give you blows at times. But, on the other hand, it may give you all the heavenly things you want. But both are unreal. Maya will keep you in an airtight situation where you believe it to be the Reality. It will make you believe that you have to play along and undergo this suffering. But once the recognition starts, you see clearly that "O! God! What have

I been doing all this time? Enough of this drama. I don't want to play this anymore." This spontaneous recognition gives you freedom. It frees you instantly from this madness.

The Upanishads tell us to see clearly that you are not a limited human being. You are That One Reality, which is the substratum of everything like the sun, that is self-effulgent, whether it be day or dusk. So, likewise, the Self is self-effulgent. That's the only Reality. The rest is all Asat. You are not the mind. The mind is only something you are aware of. Your essential nature is that of Being-Awareness. Understand that the body and mind are subject to constant change. The mind constantly experiences various sensations, thoughts, feelings, and emotions. Happiness and suffering are the nature of the mind; likewise, depression, anxiety, jealousy, pride, and other emotions are of the mind alone.

If you want to calm your mind, you can practice various spiritual disciplines to control your mind and senses. Whatever activities you find yourself engaged in, do so while maintaining the attitude that oneself is neither 'doer' nor 'enjoyer'. Increase the sattvic quality of your body and mind through consuming the right kind of food, yoga postures, contemplative practices such as japa and meditation. All these will help in developing and maintaining an equanimous state of mind (samatvam).

However, for the permanent ending of suffering, Self-knowledge is the only answer. Rest as the Self, whose nature is Being-Awareness-Bliss. The essential thing here is to know that all thoughts, sensations, perceptions and feelings are unreal in nature; they just arise and cease as they are impermanent in nature. They do not belong to the Self. The Self is Ever pure. 'Suffering is not my real nature. It's only the nature of mind, just like the nature of fire is to burn, and the nature of water is coolness.' Each has its nature, and the nature of Self is Ever Free of all body, mind, senses, intellect, and world nature.

Freedom from Samsara

A conversation regarding freedom from Samsara.

Question: As far as my body-mind complex is concerned, after gaining knowledge of Aham Brahmāsmi, I attain Mukti, which is my nature. Just like when a wave reaches the shore, it dies, but the formation of new waves continues again. Similarly, the Chaitanya may manifest in another body-mind complex and undergo Samsara until it gets Knowledge.

Thus how can we say that there is no Samsara is Atma?

Answer: Samsara is an illusion, just like a snake in a rope. That's why Advaita Vedanta says Anirvachanēya kayathi (indescribable error). It's only an appearance. So we are not saying either snake as sat (exist) or asat (non-exist).

Take the example of a rope being perceived as a snake. If the snake was real, it would always exist. Sat means something that exists in all three periods of time (past, present and future). However, we know the snake has no reality when the rope is investigated with light.

Or if we say 'asat', then like the horns of a rabbit, it should not be there at all (nonexistent), but that does not quite apply in this situation either, because someone did see the snake! So it was just an appearance at the time of illusion.

A magic show is an illusion because we cannot use the money given by the magician during the show after a magic show. After all, it is just an illusion, and we thought it to be true when the magician gave it to us.

So we are saying Samsara has no reality by itself to continue once the proper Knowledge dawns on us. It seemed to be so during ignorance. It got sublated (Bādhitha) when Knowledge about Self was recognized and realized Self as un-sublated in nature (Abādhitha is swarupa).

When we have the illusion of a separate self, we continue from one body to another. Because each time we identify with a body-mind complex, we feel it to be real, like in a dream also the feeling is there. In a dream, we have a different body-mind complex, but we are that and feel till the dream lasts as we are identified with it.

But when we go to deep sleep, we are free of the separate self-illusion of waking and dream body-mind complex. So we remain exclusively as Sat. Here we are saying as Sat (existence) alone is there in all three states. Still, we think we are limited because of our identification, so Samsara is there for me. The realization and recognition of that Sat the Self brings us to our actual state. (Ch Up 6-2-1)

Nothing happens except the recognition of Brahman the Self. So the desire to be free from samsara misery is just an illusion because we think we are bound with happiness-misery, loss-gain, etc. But in reality, Sat the Self is absolutely free all the time. This is the Truth that Upanishads declare as Brahman alone is Truth, and everything is Brahman.

Not that one Brahman is out there. For now, jiva is bound in Samsara and later by all practices on all forms and formless including (Sravana, manana..) one day attain it.

Here we are not speaking in terms of utility attitude. However, even regarding Knowledge about Brahman, we approach and calculate in utility terms and fail to see the Truth.

This type of approach itself is an illusion. Instead, there is no samsara to be liberated. No one is bound to be freed. Wholeness is Brahman, and there is no above or below, nor is there greater than Brahman.

When we limit the infinite Brahman, we get illusionary ideas like this. This is not a promissory note to say 'Brahman you will become;' 'now just don't say you are Brahman 'or 'just by saying I am Brahman, you will not become Brahman.' So, 'now you are limited, bound so do all practices realize Brahman (including Sravana, manana..).'

In that approach, Upanishads are not saying. Brahman is not somewhere to be attained, and jiva is not somewhere to reach it or attain it or realize it. So that utility way of thinking is not correct. Confusion arises when we think we should get purity to regain it.

Here Upanishads are speaking from a wholeness standpoint, and we should understand from that standpoint, not from our illusion separate self standpoint.

On the one hand, if we think we are incomplete, and on the other hand wanting to become complete is itself an illusion (Bhrama).

Truth is not confined to our concepts. We may have concepts that are a different story. But Truth as such is wholeness which is Brahman.

Upanishads clearly say that there is no samsara or jiva bound to that.

Therefore, if we have doubts regarding how day-to-day activities happen? Here we say it happens accordingly like dream activities. More or less real is only a viewpoint. All appear and cease according to their function.

The illusion of a separate self cannot arise when there is no identification with those functions we see as dreams. We cannot expect mirage waters to wet the land! It is the nature of appearance, and we don't have desires for them.

What is the course of an individual when one is leading the life in the world is not a problem when situations arise either in favor or unfavorable to one as there is no illusion of separate self-existence.

From Brahman's wholeness standpoint, there is no scope for such illusions. A Snake in the rope like that, there is no scope. Entertaining ideas which have no substance are like fairy tales.

The moment-to-moment interactions with each individual are a phenomenon without shortcomings, like an ocean. All waves, foam, and bubbles are part of that great phenomenon without an illusion being different from the wholeness.

The feeling of separateness is not a reality. See from that standpoint. Here that phenomenon is Brahman. Jiva's inert or active life force is all part of that one phenomenon called Brahman.

Therefore separate self-feeling is an illusion that has no reality apart from Brahman. Therefore, as Brahman, if we accept jiva, the individual, there is no second other than that reality Brahman. So the Upanishad's words 'Tat Twam Asi' remain ever true.

Body afflictions, mind afflictions in different situations, and proportions according to each one's karma are all happenings in the wholeness Phenomenon called Brahman. From that standpoint, nothing is happening in terms of increase-decrease, happiness-misery, etc. It is fullness (pUrna) like space or ocean.

There is no Jiva, a separate self, to claim the Brahman as it is a wholeness phenomenon. All our illusory concepts cease in the right discernment.

The problem is we retain ourselves and try to understand the Truth. But in reality, we have to give up the idea of separate self-illusion who wants freedom (Mukthi) as Brahman is ever free, Satchitananda.

A letter from a reader

Someone who happened to read the previous book wrote to me: "I enjoyed reading your book and the poems in it. Yet, I have to confess I do not understand this restlessness or insistence on understanding 'Who I am'. My perspective is that there is little reason to inquire into the purpose of life, this universe, the mysteries of life, and so on. I am happy with where I am in life, and feel like I know who I am and the purpose of my life on earth. I am content with this and feel there is no reason for me to search further. Do you have anything to say about this?"

I responded

This is not the first time someone has written or said something similar to me. It is usually something along the lines of "I am content with where I am in my life right now. I am content with what I have achieved, and the general direction my life is headed in. I have no reason to go searching for the mysteries of life, or to pursue 'my REAL Self'. After all, what purpose will Self-realization serve? You already made it clear it does not bring one more money, power and so on, nor does it help in dispelling my material problems like illnesses or financial troubles. So why should I care about Self-realization? In Fact, I can safely say I do not care for it. I am already happy enough with my life."

To this I would say

Whether one realizes it or not, what everyone essentially is doing during their entire life is the pursuit of the Self. Through every experience, through every thought, emotion or feeling, we relate to the world fundamentally seeking to define ourselves in some way or the other. Things are essential or unessential, important or unimportant, pleasant or unpleasant, a cause for happiness or suffering, all depending on how it impacts 'me'. If something impacts my sense of 'I' negatively, that is, if I feel my sense of individuality is diminished through some object, thought or experience, then it is rigidly resisted. If something expands the sense of individuality, one pursues it or clings to it with all their might. All this is done due to the love of the Self. However, since we misunderstand what this 'Self' is, and wrongly identify it with our bodies, minds and possessions, our quest to manage our sense of individuality is a never-ending one. Not only is it never ending, but it is very fragile.

Any statement like 'I know what I am already' is a pretty short-sighted one, because it is very conditional. It depends on the current state of the body-mind-world complex, like one's material possessions, money and power situation, family situation and so on. A single change could completely upset this so-called contentment. A stomach ulcer, a job promotion denied, a divorce, loss of a loved one - any such events could dramatically change how we feel about ourselves, as well as change our outlook towards life. When such things happen, people urgently seek any cures that would restore things to 'as they were before'. However, this rarely happens. Why? This is because change is the law of nature. Nature is ever-changing, and thus, any sort of security or imagined stability we have in our sense of 'I' is fragile and temporary. Real stability, contentment and security are only to be found when we divert our search in understanding our 'Self' as we really are, and not through objects and experiences.

However, most people seem unwilling to do this. Instead, we seek to keep ourselves distracted, either in material pursuits with the false belief that it will bring us lasting happiness, or in pursuing various imagined altruistic endeavors thinking it will bring us joy and fulfillment in exchange for our so-called 'good actions'. People invent various 'codes of conducts', imagine 'the purpose of life', craft different lifestyles, all with the desire to enhance their living conditions, believing that it will bring them fulfillment. One only needs to spend a few minutes browsing through any of today's social media apps to see how people invent different motivations and ascribe meanings to life's various activities. Traveling the world, building schools and hospitals, becoming a millionaire or a billionaire, growing a large family, and so on - none of these work as life strategies for providing fulfillment.

As long as one misunderstands who they are, all activities from this false center of 'self' are bound to fail. They will inevitably end in dissatisfaction and failure, causing suffering for oneself and others around them. Hence the necessity to pursue the inquiry 'Who am I?' and to understand their changeless

Self-nature. Thus far, we have all been doing this unconsciously, but now, if we pursue this quest directly, putting aside the seeking for objects and experiences, we will find that which we were indirectly seeking through these external experiences. What modern literature often calls 'Self-actualization' does not really come from materialistic pursuits. Abraham Maslow later added something called 'self transcendence' to his 'Hierarchy of needs', which is nothing but an understanding of our own true Self-nature. This is where all search ends.

Understanding one's Self-nature has nothing to do with crafting imagined ideas about oneself. The rishis of the Upanishads, through direct experience, understood, and then shared this understanding with future generations. They declare 'Tat Twam Asi', that 'One's Self is that pure Awareness.'

These Upanishads words, when one hears, reflects on and meditates diligently, then one realizes that his Self, his 'I' to be ever Free, and it is the Reality. All the limitations superimposed on 'I' get negated. This is real Self-understanding.

Lastly, there is the question of why pursue Self-enquiry when it does not bring one more money, power, etc, nor does it help in dispelling my material problems like illnesses or financial troubles. Frankly, this is because Self-realization has nothing to do with these. Self-realization is more of a corrective surgery, like the removal of cataract from the eye. With this, one understands the nature of one's Self correctly. With this understanding, one is no longer at odds with life as it is. Such a person is able to respond appropriately, without unnecessary mental turbulence to life events as they happen.

There is no conflict between our spiritual pursuit to understand our Self-nature, and in fulfilling our roles to our families and society. This was in fact the gist of Sri Krishna's advice to Arjuna in the Bhagavad Gita. He told Arjuna to act according to his dharma, while being established in his Self-nature. With such Self-abidance, one can then do the needful either in gaining money, possessions, taking care of family, or in improving one's physical health and so on.

To conclude, we need to understand that this pursuit of 'Who am I?' is not an optional aspect of our life, but in fact its very essence. Ignorance makes us unaware of our Self-nature, and makes us look for what we seek in the wrong places. To dispel such ignorance, Self-enquiry is the only way.

Meditation and food - a discussion

In the Chandogya Upanishad, the concept of purity of food is elucidated, emphasizing its deeper implications beyond mere physical nourishment.

> āhāraśuddhau sattvaśuddhau dhruvā smṛtiḥ
> smṛtilambhe sarvagranthīnāṃ vipramokṣastasmai
> mṛditakaṣāyāya tamasaspāraṃ darśayati - 7-26-2

If one eats pure food, one's mind becomes pure. If the mind is pure, one's memory becomes strong and steady. If the memory is good, one becomes free from all bondages.

It is important to expand on the qualification of the word "food". Food extends beyond its tangible form to include all sensory inputs—sound (śabda), smell (gandha), taste (rasa), vision (rūpa), touch (sparśa), and more—by the senses (indriya), mind (manas), and intellect (buddhi). When one consumes saatvik inputs, the inner understanding clears up and eventually one comes to remember the Truth regarding one's Self nature, and thus becomes free from all bondages.

Yet, the food one eats has an inordinate impact on sadhana, specifically the ability to still one's mind during meditation, as well as to be mindful during activity. For meditation, a moderate diet can be conducive to supporting mental clarity, focus, and overall well-being.

Sri Krishna also instructs Arjuna on the importance of this topic in the 6:17 of the Bhagavad Gita. That particular chapter of the Gita is focused on the path of attaining freedom through meditation.

Yuktāhara-viharasya Yukta-cestasya karmasu
Yukta-svapnāvabodhasya Yogo bhavati duhkha-hā

Yoga becomes the destroyer of sorrow for one whose eating and movements are regulated, whose effort in work is moderate, and whose sleep and wakefulness are temperate.

In this verse, Lord Krishna emphasizes the significance of moderation and balance in all aspects of life, including dietary habits. Just as one should practice moderation in activities such as eating, sleeping, and working, a balanced diet forms an integral part of this lifestyle. Following a diet that is moderate and balanced aligns with the principles of yoga outlined in the Gita. It involves consuming wholesome, nourishing foods in appropriate quantities, avoiding overindulgence or excessive restriction. Such a diet supports overall health and well-being, enabling individuals to maintain physical vitality and mental clarity.

Some general guidelines on what foods are helpful to a life devoted to meditation and sadhana are outlined below. One must reflect on one's health, the amount of activity their duties require and follow a diet that best suits them.

Plant-Based Whole Foods: Base your diet on plant-based whole foods, including fruits, vegetables, legumes, whole grains, nuts, and seeds. These foods are rich in essential nutrients, fiber, and antioxidants, which support overall health and vitality.

Fresh Fruits and Vegetables: Incorporate a variety of fresh fruits and vegetables into your meals and snacks. These colorful foods provide vitamins, minerals, and phytonutrients that nourish the body and promote optimal brain function.

Whole Grains: Choose whole grains such as brown rice, quinoa, oats, barley, and whole wheat. Whole grains are a good source of complex carbohydrates, which provide sustained energy and help maintain stable blood sugar levels, supporting focus and concentration during meditation.

Plant-Based Proteins: Include plant-based protein sources such as beans, lentils, chickpeas, tofu, tempeh, and edamame. These protein-rich foods provide essential amino acids necessary for neurotransmitter synthesis and support muscle repair and maintenance.

Healthy Fats: Incorporate healthy fats into your diet from sources such as avocados, nuts, seeds, olive oil, and coconut oil. These fats support brain health and cognitive function, enhancing mental clarity and focus during meditation.

Herbs and Spices: Use herbs and spices to add flavor to your meals without relying on excessive salt or unhealthy seasonings. Herbs and spices like turmeric, ginger, cinnamon, and basil not only enhance the taste of dishes but also offer potential health benefits, including anti-inflammatory and antioxidant properties.

Hydration: Stay well-hydrated by drinking plenty of water throughout the day. Proper hydration supports optimal brain function and helps maintain mental alertness and focus during meditation sessions.

Practice mindful eating: Eat by paying attention to the flavors, textures, and sensations of the food you consume. Eat slowly, chew thoroughly, and savor each bite, fostering a deeper connection to your body and promoting a sense of presence and awareness. Bring all your senses into awareness so that you stay in the here and now, which is utmost necessary for meditation. As you bring awareness to all aspects of your body-mind-senses-intellect, meditation becomes as natural as it is, without any obstacles. Remember, you have never truly left the Self; it is just a matter of recognizing it in the light of that awareness.

Last thing to note regarding food, is that it is also not just what one eats, but also how the food is handled. The concept of consecrated food or 'prasād' is one many of us are familiar with. Foods handled with a sātvic state of mind, with an attitude of offering to the divine, are aids to meditation.

By adopting a disciplined approach to diet and lifestyle, individuals can mitigate material pains and cultivate a sense of harmony and balance within themselves. This balanced approach to nutrition not only supports the practice of yoga but also contributes to the cultivation of inner peace and spiritual growth.

The Individual Is Never Really There, Only The Self Is Present

Swami:

Can one remain devoid of thought for a while? After listening to what I am going to tell you, see if you can grasp the Truth that your real nature is Atman and be without thoughts for a while.

One day at the bus stand in Davanagere (a town in Karnataka, India), a person was behaving just like the Kannada movie actor Raj Kumar. He was singing, gesturing, and speaking just like the movie actor and was imitating him in every way. Folks at the bus stand understood that he was a beggar and gave him some money. Others standing there felt that he was a mental case and called an ambulance. The ambulance came and he was taken to a hospital. Even with the doctor at the hospital, this man was behaving just like Raj Kumar and mentioned to him that he was none other than Raj Kumar. Despite the psychiatrist asking him if he could feel that he was not Raj Kumar, at least for a few seconds, he continued to say that he was Raj Kumar.

During this time, Amritachit Swami was in the psychiatry ward as part of his clinical rotation in his medical college when the doctor started the treatment for this patient. The treatment consisted of the doctor continuing to ask the patient every day if he could feel that he was not Raj Kumar, at least for a few seconds. The doctor asked the patient to practice having the thought that he was not Raj Kumar for at least a few seconds every day, along with medication.

After three days, he started for a few seconds one day to faintly remember that he was someone else. Then, a few days after that, his memory came back and he told the doctor his real name and that he was from Chitradurga, a place in Karnataka. The doctor contacted the patient's parents and the police, and there was a reunion in which the parents told the doctor that he was watching too many movies of Raj Kumar, and when they scolded him, he left home and had this mental episode.

Similarly, we have to understand our real nature. We all feel that we are individual selves with names and forms. Can we be without thoughts, at least for a few seconds? The Scriptures and the Guru clearly tell us that due to our identification with the body-mind complex, we continue to think that we are individual selves. In reality, the sadhaka (student) himself/herself is the Atman (Self).

The Scriptures tell us that we are the Atman and not the individual self. So slowly, we have to introduce the thought that our real nature is the Self (Atman). We should not focus on what we are thinking and feeling but on what the Scriptures and Guru are saying. Our nature is always free and without limitation. It is truly the Atman, the Universal Being. The very moment we hear the teaching, we should destroy the ignorance of our real nature. It is really as simple as that. The individual is never really there; only the Self is present. The wave is a superimposition on the ocean water. The wave at any given time is water only, and it never really existed separate from water. The case of the individual (person) is exactly the same. It never existed, and its existence is only an illusion. The Self alone is imagined as the Jiva (the individual self).

Discussion

Question: Even as you are speaking about this, I feel that oneness and am able to see the individual dissolving and the feeling of oneness permeating.

Swami: Yes, it is like morning mist. As soon as the light falls on the vapor, it disappears. There is really no discussion about the Jiva (individual) because the Jiva never existed.

The real sadhana is knowing our true nature. There is really no Jiva, only a lack of recognition of our real nature. That is why understanding immediately dissolves the individual, and only the presence of the Atman remains. Just as the patient was imagining he was Raj Kumar while all the time being himself, he was never Raj Kumar but himself all the time. Similarly, there is only the Atman all the time, and this Jivahood is only a superimposition on it caused by ignorance. Due to ignorance of his real nature, he thinks he is the individual while being the Atman all the time.

With the knowledge that he is the Atman, the illusion of Jivahood is exposed. Basically, the Self knows itself. The illusion of a separate self is exposed. In Para drishti (outward standpoint), you feel the individual and the world, but with Swarupa drishti (Self standpoint), there is really nothing other than the Atman. The one who is actually the Atman is imagining that he is the individual. The Self is really knowing itself, and at the same time, it itself is appearing as the world due to ignorance.

There is no question of moving from Jivahood to Atman. The Jivahood is never there. It is just a deception. Reality is actually free of thoughts, but thoughts are an imagination on the Truth. The purpose of knowledge is to remove ignorance and expose the illusory feeling of a separate self. By "Tat Tvam Asi" means that there was never any Jiva (individual), but only the Self.

There is no other scriptural Truth to say that you are not the Self. Doubts arise as long as there is no firm understanding, but once the firm conviction comes, the sense of the individual dissolves and only the Atman is seen in its place.

There is no question of further practice once the knowledge comes. The subject is the real nature of the person, which has always been the Atman.

Question: Can we say that there is nothing else other than the Atman?

Swami: Yes. Knowledge removes the ignorance of the student and shows that his real nature is the Atman.

Question: Can we say that ignorance is resolving (dissolving) itself in the Self?

Swami: Yes. There is not really any ignorance separately. It exists only as long as you don't know the Truth. The minute you know the Truth the ignorance dissolves because it never really exists. The individual never really existed at any point.

Question: Does this knowledge get covered up again once after understanding? Do we feel that we are individuals again after once getting this understanding?

Swami: - Once there is a firm conviction that you are the Atman, there is no way that the sense of the individual can come back.

Question: In Jivan Mukti Viveka Swami Vidyaranya, mentions about a final step of Jivan Mukti (full realization) as the destruction of the mind (mano nasa)

Swami: Here, we are not leaving anything on the table. Once the conviction comes, there is nothing else to be done. The ignorance never comes back.

Question: Is it possible to get this kind of 100% conviction that we are the Self just by listening?

Swami: Why not? Absolutely, we can get 100% convinced if we understand it fully. The very root of ignorance is destroyed. Sravanath Jnanam, Jnanath Mukthi (from listening comes knowledge, and from knowledge comes liberation). Our thoughts and memories of being an individual have to be brought to closure through this understanding, and all memories have to be illuminated through this new understanding, and then all sorrow resulting from old memories will be destroyed. For example, when a child falls, she will cry at that time, and then again the next day she will remember it and say that she fell down and will continue to do that for a few days. Only when the mother takes the child to the spot where she fell down and gives a beating to the spot will the child feel satisfied and get closure for her memory of the injury. Similarly, we need to illuminate all our hurtful memories through this new understanding, and then the memory, even though it will continue, will not be painful because it has been illumined with the new understanding that there is only the Self and nothing else. Similarly, when a Sanyasi gets a new name, the old name will continue to exist but become faint and of no consequence. The world will continue to be as usual, but its reality will be illumined by the knowledge of the Self and so it will lose its sting and appear like a dream.

Sruti (Scripture), Yukti (logical discussions, satsangs) and anubhavam (one's own experience) point out that there is nothing other than the Self.

Obstacles to freedom

When one listens to the scriptural declarations that the Self is ever free, of the nature of Being-Awareness-Bliss and nothing exists outside of the Self, one often wonders why their natural experience is so different. If 'Maya', which is cosmic illusion, means something 'that does not exist', then why are we not free? Why do we not realize our Self-nature here and now?

There was a discussion on this topic during a satsang.

Question: What are the obstacles for spiritual progress?

Answer:Traditionally, there are two kinds of obstacles one encounters on the path to Self-knowledge. The first type obstructs the attainment of knowledge (Jnana Utpathi), and the second type hinders one from becoming firm in that knowledge (Jnana Phalam).

Jnana Utpathi: Obstacles to Gaining Knowledge

When trying to study the shastras (scriptures) or listen to teachings, various obstacles may arise. For example, you might get distracted or not understand the topic during a scriptural class. This happens due to a lack of purity in the mind (chitta suddhi), which prevents understanding. To overcome this obstacle, we need to practice bhakti (devotion) and karma yoga (selfless action).

Karma yoga is challenging because it requires letting go of the sense of doership, the belief that actions are done by me. But, the Self (Atman) is free of action, but without conviction, we cannot develop non-doership (Akartha) and non-enjoyership (Aboktha). Since we lack this conviction, we practice bhavana (visualizing that we are the Self). Gradually, this practice helps us develop discernment (viveka) to distinguish between what is real and unreal. Recognizing the unreal leads to automatic dispassion (vairagya).

When we have the false attitudes of doership and enjoyership, it shows that we lack viveka, vairagya, mind control (sama), and sense control (dama). Without these qualities, the desire to know the Self (mumuksatvam) is weak, making it difficult to study the scriptures. Viveka, Vairagya, Sama, and Dama all create the right environment for knowledge to arise. They bring purity of mind (chitta shuddhi) and one-pointedness (chitta ekagrata), which naturally lead to seeking the Master and knowing the Self. These practices prepare the mind to receive scriptural knowledge. At this point, the seeds of knowledge are planted, but the fruit (jnana phalam) has yet to come.

Obstacles to Jnana Phalam: Firmness in Self-Knowledge

Ajnanam (ignorance) – Mistaking ourselves for the body. To remove this obstacle, we must listen to scriptures (Sravana).

This is like lighting a lamp in a dark room, which removes darkness (ajnana).

Samshaya (doubt) – Doubts about our True Nature can arise after hearing the scriptures. For example, the scriptures tell us we are the Self, but we doubt this because we still think we are the body and mind. We address this through reflection (manana), using logic (yukti) to understand our True Nature better.

Viparyaya (opposite thinking) – Misinterpreting scriptural texts because we believe we are the body/mind. To overcome this, we must contemplate and meditate on the Self (nididhyasana), recognizing it as ever-present (nitya), ever pure (suddha), ever conscious (buddha), and ever free (mukta). This contemplation turns the logic from manana into firm conviction.

Once these obstacles are cleared, the fruit of knowledge, which is liberation (mukti), is attained. It's important to note that sravana, manana, and nididhyasana happen simultaneously. For example, when someone asks you to bring tea, listening and understanding happen together, and there are no doubts about what was asked.

Question: Please give some examples to explain to illustrate misidentification and how to overcome it

Answer: A good illustration of this was a brahmachari who had a recent head injury that led to amnesia. As he had forgotten who he was, Amma (the Guru) reminded him repeatedly of his name. He was like a newborn, who, when born, doesn't have full awareness of limbs, etc., but that doesn't negate that he/she has them. Non-comprehension (Vedanta calls this non-apprehension) of Self is the common thread between this brahmachari and a newborn. We also have this non-apprehension as we don't know our True Nature though it exists, so we have mis-apprehension (mis-identification) that we are the body/mind. This is similar to the story of the 10th man, in which a man counted all the people except himself and kept worrying about where the 10th man was.

In another anecdote, there was once a young prince of a kingdom which suddenly came under attack. For his safety, the prince was taken away by the minister to a far-away forest and was given to forest dwellers to raise. Years went by, and the young boy grew up into a young man, believing he was a forest dweller, unaware of his True Nature. After the war was resolved, the minister was sent to bring the prince back to the kingdom. When the minister arrived and explained to the young man that he was actually a prince, the prince doubted this. The minister then went through great lengths to convince him of his True Nature, and the prince finally believed (key word) that he was actually a prince. After coming back to the kingdom, he was re-acquainted with his family and started to understand that he was actually a prince. However, as he had lived for so many years with the identity of the forest dweller, the prince would sometimes doubt his princehood, and the minister would again gently explain to him his True Nature.

Question: Swami, sometimes when I start to understand this scriptural knowledge, I notice that the likes and dislikes of the body mind level do not disappear and, in fact, sometimes increase. How does one sublimate this part of the ego?

Swami: Don't be judgmental while gaining this knowledge. Everything has a place, and you need to make sure to put everything in the right place. As Amma says, even a small screw in the airplane plays an important role. Everything has a place, which is why it's here in this galaxy. If you give the right place for everything, then prejudice and aversion won't arise. If someone makes a bad comment, you keep it in the right place and let it flow. You should be like a traffic policeman who guides thoughts to their right place. Currently, what we are doing is jumbling everything from a body-mind standpoint.

When you are aware of your true Self nature, it's not like the body and mind disappear. You just don't brood over it. Once you have the conviction that you are the Self, you become the traffic controller and give the right place to your mind and body so they aren't neglected and won't trouble you. This way, the potential to overpower your self-realization won't be there. Another way to think about it is that we are giving a nice space for the body-mind but at the same time, it's like a dog in a nice kennel, and it's clear who the master is. We don't have any aversion to mirages (our own body, mind, and others as well), but everything goes in the kennel, so we remain undisturbed.

Spirituality does not mean we are against comforts, but we are putting them in their right place so we don't have the illusion that they will give us everlasting peace. A simple example is that we eat food, but we understand that the food we are eating now will not give us permanent happiness. These things won't dictate to you, as they don't have an unchanging reality to dictate to you.

However, as your body mind interacts with other body minds, you need to take care of their needs even after recognizing them from an Atman standpoint. If you go to jewelry shop with a lot of gold ornaments, the owner knows, for example, that anklets are worn on the ankle and not on the neck. That is the wisdom of the Atman standpoint. This illusory world does not carry you away.

Where do likes and dislikes arise from? It arises from ignorance of your True Nature. The Self does not hate (na dvesti) or desire (na kanshati). Through sravana, we listen to our Self Nature and recognize it.

Question: During meditation, I often struggle with reaching a meditative, thoughtless state, and forcibly trying to calm my thoughts is often a temporary solution. What advice would you give someone starting to meditate?

Swami:

When you see it from the Self standpoint, you are naturally free of thoughts. When you take the Tattwajnana (self-knowledge) standpoint, you are free. Attempting to meditate and waiting for the gap in thoughts to increase from a body mind standpoint is futile, as you create resistance by giving false importance to your thoughts. There is a tendency to "concentrate" on our Self Nature but it is important to realize that we are also struggling from a body mind standpoint. Chitta vritthi nirodha (forcibly holding your thoughts), which is stipulated by Yoga, tries to control the body and mind in an abrupt fashion. This may succeed or fail.

Instead, recognizing your Self Nature (pratyabhijna - prati- ("re-") + abhi- ("closely") + jna ("to know"), whose meaning is "direct knowledge of one's Self," "recognition"), which is naturally free of thoughts, is a more direct path.

In the previous satsang, there was the story of a psychiatric patient who thought he was a famous actor named Rajkumar. The psychiatrist would ask daily Is there a time when you don't feel you are Rajkumar (mis-identification)? What the psychiatrist tried to elucidate was whether there was a time he was thinking from his original personality and not asking the fake personality of Rajkumar, was there any time that the fake personality feels there is a gap? Similarly, we care about our Self Nature while meditating, not our body mind standpoint.

Question: What does Tat Twam Asi (Thou art that) mean?

Swami: Space is the substratum in which everything exists. As you look closely at these objects that occupy space, space still exists even between atoms. This space is actually one continuous substratum, in which the body-mind exist as well. There may be many bodies, but there is only one Atman. When this body mind dissolves, did the Atman disappear as well?No, as the Atman has no place to go as it is all-pervasive. If a small butterfly flies in the sky, is the sky affected? No. Similarly in the Atman, the body mind sense complex arise, sustain, and dissolve in the Self

Nature. The activities of the body mind complex won't affect the Self Nature. But due to our ignorance the appearance of the body mind seems to real. Self-realization is not something where you become like the Atman and the world interactions disappear. By understanding the Self Nature and the illusory nature of this body mind, you are in meditation 24 hours a day. Meditation is not a word or process, it is a beingness and knowingness.

8. Meditations on Self-nature

The Final Nail in The Coffin

There is no choice regarding awareness of one's nature because it is the only reality seen in everything. In fact, "Sat" is the essence and presence where all is revealed. Thoughts, sensations, perceptions, and feelings are sensed and aware within it. Freedom is what allows everything to find its place. It is Nitya Muktha (ever-free), Anantam (infinite), Nirupadika (attribute-less), and Purnam (wholeness). The key to this choiceless freedom lies in its unconditional nature. This is what Sruti means when it says "Nitya" (ever-present), "Suddha" (unblemished), "Buddha" (ever-conscious), and "Muktha" (ever-free). In all these definitions, Atma (the Self) is described as untainted and detached to anything because it is inherently Mukthi (ever-free). When one feels limited and bound, it is merely an imagination where limitations are superimposed on the unlimited. "Why" is the question, and "why not" is the answer because it has the freedom to imagine itself with birth, sustenance, and death. In the realm of presence, everything happens without choice. It is similar to a boat on the surface of water, rather than water getting inside the boat.

This presence exists prior to the mind-body-world complex, much like deep sleep, where it is exclusive oneness and the only essence. It represents unconditional freedom. Similarly, unconditional freedom is present in the waking state. It witnesses all appearances and disappearances without losing its consciousness effulgence. Overall, freedom alone expresses itself through names and forms in the waking state, while freedom alone remains in deep sleep. This reveals that freedom alone is the absolute reality, which is to say that Brahman alone is the absolute truth. Everything else is like passing clouds without specific definitions, and the presence enables all happenings as phenomena, while Brahman is unconditional, infinite wholeness. If a feeling arises, to whom does this feeling come? We often say, "to me" or "I." But who is this "me" or "I"? When a feeling comes, it eventually leaves, indicating the different expressions of thoughts, sensations, perceptions, and feelings. What is it that senses, makes us aware, and lets us know about these experiences? It is the intrinsic nature upon which these experiences arise and cease, making way for new ones. This intrinsic nature, upon which everything comes and goes, cannot be defined because all definitions themselves are sensed, made aware of, and known.

Therefore, it cannot be known, sensed, perceived, or felt. Instead, in the presence of That, all things have a temporary sense of existence but are soon replaced, much like waves in an ocean. That which enables all phenomena or happenings is choiceless awareness, often mistaken for having a choice, leading us to attempt to relive the past or imagine a future. This construct is woven or wired into our beliefs, making us think we are free beings to think and act. However, this is not the case, as everything is being made aware in the presence. In reality, freedom intrinsically expresses itself, but we attempt to label and condition it according to our choices. This is a fundamental error or ignorance, much like constructing a palace of clouds, shaping clouds, and naming them, only to realize that they disintegrate before our eyes.

Creation, sustenance, and destruction are not ultimate realities; they are impermanent in nature and ultimately fall apart. All these phenomena find their presence in the unconditional nature, which is wholeness - Brahman, the absolute reality. As

"I," it expresses and effulges as the Self, Atma, not as anatma, the non-self. Therefore, everything possesses the presence of That rather than having its own independent existence. Feelings are sensed within That presence, but not by an individual, because there is no individual entity to claim the feelings. The awareness itself is often mistaken for an individual, and thus the ego is recognized as a fictional entity, lacking substantiality. Brahman alone is the ultimate reality, and the recognition of this with viveka, discernment, as instructed by Sruti (scriptures), becomes the ultimate authority, establishing it as the unblemished reality.

When we say Choiceless Awareness is intrinsic in nature, it is not something created but the very essence of Being and Knowing. Thoughts, sensations, perceptions, and feelings are known just like objects such as tables and chairs, but they do not transform into 'I am.' In this Awareness, they are not actions but rather illuminate, much like how light illuminates a room. The nature of Awareness is like that of light, which shines as itself and not as objects. When we turn on the light, it is the light alone, yet we superimpose the perception of seeing things to avoid bumping into objects. Similarly, Choiceless Awareness functions as its own nature. It is not merely a witness but is inherently effulgent, embodying Being-Knowing-Bliss in an exclusive oneness. This alone is the Absolute Truth, while everything else is an appearance without substantiality.

"The final nail in the coffin" is what "Tat twam asi" stands for. It signifies that choiceless awareness is your nature, as well as the nature of everything else. It does not attach itself to a name or form but expresses itself intrinsically, much like the beauty of a flower, as Amma explains: "Does the beauty and fragrance of a flower exist solely within that flower? No, that is not the case. It does not unfold in such a limited way. Beauty and fragrance do not reside as mere aspects of the intrinsic essence of nature confined within the form and shape of an object or a person.

Rather, beauty is an expression of the intrinsic essence of nature that transcends names and forms. Even if the physical form ceases to exist, the beauty within the intrinsic essence of nature remains undiminished. Similarly, love is an inner facet of the intrinsic essence of nature, impervious to destruction. It does not exist within the boundaries of names and forms. Therefore, that love which permeates everyone and everything, surpassing the realms of intellect and thought, enduring eternally, represents the inner Truth that must be experienced and shared with others." - Amma The withering of a flower while its beauty remains intact serves as a metaphor for the eternal nature of true beauty, often referred to as 'Satyam Shivam Sundaram.'"

Amma's example of the withering flower carries a deep spiritual insight. The physical form of the flower may fade and wither away, but its essential beauty remains untouched by the passage of time. This observation draws a parallel to the concept of "Satyam Shivam Sundaram," where truth (Satyam), divinity (Shivam), and beauty (Sundaram) are seen as one exclusive in nature and eternal aspects of existence.

The flower's essence, its intrinsic beauty, serves as a reminder that genuine beauty transcends the temporary and impermanent aspects of the material world. It points to the timeless nature of inner beauty, which exists beyond surface appearance. In this context, "Satyam Shivam Sundaram" encapsulates the idea that truth, divinity, and beauty are inseparable and form the core essence of all existence.

The teaching emphasizes that while the world may be full of appearances and transient forms, it is essential to recognize and focus on the eternal truth that underlies everything. In the grand scheme of things, all else is mere illusion or a passing mirage. The flower, in its withering, beautifully illustrates the impermanence of the physical world and the enduring nature of the spiritual and beautiful essence that lies within.

Thus, we can see the limitations of thoughts, sensations, perceptions, and feelings. The ego, which identifies with the body-mind-world complex and is entangled in Samsara, requires discernment to recognize, as stated by Sruti. It is not a process for breaking free; rather, it is choiceless awareness that enables us to recognize when we hear Sruti. Awareness has nothing to do with these, much like a dream when waking occurs. Therefore, awareness is choiceless, similar to illumination, as it is the Swabhav (intrinsic nature) and not an imposed superimposition. "That Brahman you are" represents the final realization of this truth.

Exploring the Depths of Awareness

Sit with your fears and anxieties in full Awareness. Acknowledge them fully. Give undivided attention to them while maintaining a state of heightened Awareness. Be present with them, observing their every nuance. Slowly, they may reveal answers, or they may not. However, don't approach them with the expectation of finding a solution. The key is to simply be with them, to face them head-on, all while being fully Aware of their presence. Avoid labeling them as good or bad, just observe them closely with unwavering Awareness. This practice of watching and truly seeing fears and anxieties with Awareness provides immense strength. Instead of hiding them away, allow them the space to exist within the realm of Awareness. That is the secret of this exercise. By giving them the space to be, you are recognizing them without judgment or suppression in the light of Awareness.

So, the exercise of sitting with fears and anxieties, and giving them your presence, Awareness, and attention, allows a deeper understanding of oneself and the discovery of inner strength. In this way, the observer, the observed, and Awareness itself become one, transcending duality and finding unity within. In this Awareness, all thoughts, sensations, perceptions, feelings are not you. You are no more defined by them. You are not an identity tag with all these. Instead, you are Aware presence where they appear or may not, but they don't have the reality of themselves to define themselves. Instead, they look to Awareness to feed them. This game has been played time immemorial, so the burden of memory and repetitive behavioral patterns say one is trapped in them, unable to free from them. As we clearly see, they fade in the presence of Awareness. They get healed akin to curing illness, as health is one's condition upon which illness eclipsed, so treatment is for illness.

Similarly, ignorance about the Aware Self is the cause of illness where the mind takes over with all thoughts, sensations, perceptions, feelings. But in the presence of Awareness, they heal as they are appearances that arise and cease continuously, as long as they are fed and acknowledged by taking reality from identification. So, by Awareness Presence, they get sublated, faded, as they don't have a substance to prove their presence, as unawareness has no place in Awareness. The whole thing is not action-oriented but remains As Awareness, which is the essence, content, and substratum of Self that cannot be otherwise recognized.

Understanding Awareness as the Intrinsic Nature

Awareness is often described as the intrinsic nature of thoughts and the mind itself. Unlike the quality of thoughts, which can vary widely, awareness remains constant and unchanging.

Awareness is not determined by the specific content or quality of thoughts. It is not limited to particular thoughts or mental states. Instead, it pervades all thoughts, emotions, and mental experiences. It is the very essence of the mind's activity. While thoughts and emotions can vary in quality, intensity, and content, awareness itself remains untouched by these variations. It is like an unchanging backdrop against which the diverse thoughts of the mind play out. In the context of consciousness and awareness, "Swarupam" refers to its inherent nature. Awareness is not something added to the mind; it is what the mind fundamentally is. It is the substratum upon which mental activities unfold. Awareness is often likened to space, which accommodates everything within it, from galaxies to tiny particles. Similarly, awareness accommodates all mental phenomena, from the most profound insights to the most trivial thoughts, without being limited or defined by them.

Just as space remains undivided by the objects it contains, awareness remains undivided by the multitude of thoughts and experiences it holds. It is limitless, transcending the boundaries of individual thoughts or perceptions. Recognizing awareness as the unchanging nature of the mind can lead to a sense of inner stillness and peace. It allows one to observe thoughts and emotions without getting entangled in their fluctuations. Awareness is not determined by the varying qualities of thoughts; instead, it is the unchanging and intrinsic nature of the mind itself. Understanding this nature of awareness can lead to greater clarity, equanimity, and a deeper sense of self-awareness.

Understanding Awareness as Self-Effulgence

Awareness is often described as self-effulgent and intrinsic to everything, transcending actions, thoughts, and the complexities of the body-mind-world complex. Awareness does not engage in actions, nor does it possess any special status or qualities. It simply exists, unmodified and unenhanced by anything external. Its nature is one of pure presence. This pure beingness is synonymous with the Self. In its essence, awareness is both the knower and the known. It doesn't transform or undergo modifications; it remains as it is. All transient phenomena, including thoughts and mental states, are like passing clouds in the sky of awareness. They arise, stay for a while, and eventually dissolve, leaving no lasting trace. Awareness remains unaffected, like the unchanging sky. In the absence of self-awareness and knowledge regarding the nature of awareness, the mind and its thoughts may appear to overpower and govern one's experience. However, with the wisdom derived from Sruti (sacred scriptures), one realizes that awareness is the foundation of all experiences and not a product of the mind or thoughts. Awareness is not a result of any action or process; it is inherent and uncreated. It exists prior to, during, and after any experience. It is not something that can be manufactured; it is the essential nature of everything. Awareness is not an experience in the conventional sense. Experiences come and go, but awareness remains constant. It is not subject to the ebb and flow of sensations, emotions, or thoughts. It is the very backdrop against which all experiences unfold. Awareness is self-effulgent, meaning it shines by its own light. It is not dependent on external factors for illumination. In realizing awareness as one's true nature, there is a profound sense of inner bliss, unconditioned by external circumstances or experiences.Awareness is the self-effulgent and intrinsic nature of everything, including the Self. It transcends actions, experiences, and the complexities of the mind and body. Recognizing awareness as the unchanging foundation of existence leads to a deeper understanding of one's true nature and a profound sense of inner bliss.

Progressive Awareness

In the practice of meditation, one can begin by directing their attention to any object, be it the palm of their hand, the rhythm of their breath, or the thoughts that arise. The key is to observe without attachment, recognizing that these objects are not defining the true Self but vying for attention. By adopting a discerning perspective, gradually, the focus shifts from external objects to the body, then to the mind, and ultimately to the breath and the state of pure awareness. In this state, the individual simply "is" without disturbance because awareness is infinite and unchanging. When one returns to the external world, everything appears illuminated, much like turning on a light in a room, but awareness itself cannot be defined by any object; it is the content and substratum of all experiences. So, awareness, as both Being and Knowing, defies definition by any body-mind-world complex, becoming the very essence of the reader contemplating this wisdom of the Upanishads.

Infinite Presence of Awareness

When we delve into the realm of Awareness, it's crucial not to misconstrue it as something we need to actively pursue, unlike our day-to-day activities that demand our attention. This is where the essence of true Awareness lies. Much like how we attend to our routine tasks, attending to Self-Awareness isn't about reaching a finite endpoint through meditation, scripture reading, or prayers to Guru or God. Awareness is wholeness, akin to the ocean, which is ever-fullness, the truth of wholeness.

So is the Guru. Self-Awareness is an ever-unfolding, timeless presence, consistently blossoming in the here and now. It defies the constraints of time and lacks a continuous process because it doesn't exist within the boundaries of time. It's not an object that occupies space; instead, it illuminates all within its presence. The presence we attend to signifies discernment, the realization that nothing exists outside of Awareness. There is no "inside" or "outside" to Awareness, nor does it have a specific direction, much like the unconditioned flame of a candle that illuminates without restriction. Awareness is inherently unconditional, untouched by Upadhis, limiting adjuncts and making it the Nirupadhika Truth. Your true nature is Awareness itself, and with discernment, you come to recognize that you have always existed, eternally conscious, inherently pure, and are forever liberated.

The Illusion of Separation

In day to day human experience, the ego weaves a complex narrative, often driven by the illusion of separation. It is a profound paradox that the more we perceive ourselves as separate entities, distinct from the world around us, the more we isolate ourselves from the very essence of existence. This isolation is the ego's playground, where it seeks fulfillment through myriad pursuits, only to find itself entangled and lost in the labyrinth of its own making. The ego, in its relentless quest for fulfillment, pursues external validations and accumulations, believing that they hold the key to inner contentment. It clamors for recognition, wealth, and power, thinking that these will fill the void it perceives within. Yet, as it traverses this path of materialism, it becomes increasingly evident that the satisfaction it seeks remains elusive.

The ego's endeavors are akin to a thirsty traveler in a mirage-filled desert, chasing shimmering pools of water that forever recede into the distance. It is a pursuit characterized by restlessness and never-ending desire, a cycle that perpetuates suffering. The more we cling to these illusions of fulfillment, the deeper we plunge into the abyss of confusion and despair. In this state of egoic entanglement, we often find ourselves disconnected from the deeper currents of life. We lose touch with the beings and the unity that underlies existence. The ego, in its fixation on individuality, blinds us to the profound truth that we are not separate from the world but integral parts of it. The path to transcending the ego's illusion of separation lies in self-awareness and recognition. It calls for a profound shift in perspective, a shift from ego-centeredness to a recognition of our essential oneness with all that is. It invites us to look within, to inquire into the nature of the self, and to question the validity of our perceived separateness. From a non-dual perspective, we come to understand that fulfillment does not reside in external acquisitions but in recognizing the unity of all existence. We realize that the ego's pursuits are but shadows, transient and insubstantial. True fulfillment arises when we relinquish the ego's grip on our consciousness and surrender. As we let go of the illusion of separation, we find liberation. We no longer need to chase after external validations or strive relentlessly for accumulation. Instead, we discover a deep and abiding peace within ourselves, a peace that arises from the recognition that we are an integral thread in the existence. Therefore, the ego's perpetuation of separation is the root cause of its relentless pursuit of fulfillment. However, this pursuit often leads to confusion and suffering. So, using a non-dual perspective and recognizing our inherent oneness, we can transcend the ego's illusion and find true fulfillment in the unity that underlies all of existence.

Amma's Wisdom

Unveiling the Illusion of Ignorance, Desire, and Action"

In the profound realm of Amma's love and compassion, tears often become the sacred offering that cleanses our inner being. It is said that if tears were the sole means of purging our souls, a lifetime of weeping would still seem fleeting in the grandeur of existence. This is a testament to the depth of Amma's love, which knows no bounds and accepts our tears as a precious offering.

To shed tears is to peel away layers of ignorance, to clear the veil that obscures our true understanding. Tears can be a profound expression of the Self awakening, a sign that the heart is beginning to see the inherent oneness. Each tear carries away a fragment of the ego, washing away the misconceptions that separate us from the ultimate reality.

When we cry, we often do so because we are touched by an intense emotion—grief, joy, compassion, or love. These emotions break through the hard shells of our ignorance, revealing a glimpse of our true nature and the oneness of all Being.

In those moments of vulnerability, we are closer to recognizing the divine unity which is intrinsic nature.

This recognition is more than an intellectual understanding; it is a felt experience, a deep knowing that transcends words. It is the realization that we are not isolated individuals whole, and immutable.

The tears we shed are both a release and a revelation, helping us to move beyond our limited perceptions and recognize the boundless reality of oneness.

In this state of awareness, the distinctions between Self and otherness collapse. We see ourselves in others and others in ourselves. The compassion that arises from this understanding is boundless, leading us to act with greater kindness, empathy, and love. Shedding tears becomes a sacred act, a purification that brings us closer to our true selves and to the divine essence that pervades the universe.

Thus, to shed tears is to embark on a journey of inner transformation, peeling away the layers of ignorance that obscure our vision, and ultimately, recognizing the inherent oneness of all things.

Arjuna's tears, which initially symbolize his ignorance and despair, ultimately lead to his enlightenment. By shedding these tears and receiving Krishna's teachings, Arjuna moves beyond his limited perceptions and recognizes the inherent oneness of all things. This journey from ignorance to knowledge reflects the broader spiritual path that each individual must traverse.

mayy eva mana ādhatsva mayi buddhiṁ niveśhaya

Fix the mind on Me alone; in Me alone rest the intellect. There is no doubt that hereafter you will dwell in Me alone.
– Bhagavad Gita 12:8:

Verse emphasizes the importance of devotion, equanimity, and understanding the true nature of the Self. It teaches that through faith, reflection, and the guidance of a Guru, one can transcend the illusions of duality and realize the ultimate reality of Brahman.

Our existence is intertwined with the ebb and flow of attention. Things in our lives demand our focus, and in return, they nourish us. The extent of joy we derive from these interactions depends on the depth of our engagement. The more attention we invest, the more these facets of our lives become our reality. The intricate dance of ignorance, desire, and action shapes the narrative of our existence. When we step away from the present moment and wander into the labyrinth of desires, we inadvertently enter the realm of ignorance. Desires, like unseen puppeteers, pull the strings, compelling us to engage in various actions that perpetuate a never-ending cycle. The root of this cycle lies in ignorance, specifically ignorance of the Self. Our separation from the true essence of our being triggers desires, which in turn lead to actions. In this way, we find ourselves entangled in the world, trapped within the confines of our body-mind complex. We assume different roles and identities, much like donning various masks, and from this interplay, the world as we know it springs forth. In this intricate web of existence, the grammar of life often remains elusive. We become actors on the stage of life, entangled in the drama of desires and actions.

Yet, Amma's teachings illuminate the path to break free from this cycle, guiding us towards self-realization and lliberation. Amma's wisdom invites us to return to the present moment, to shed the layers of ignorance, and to recognize the inherent oneness of all things. By doing so, we unveil the illusion of separation and release the grip of desires and actions. In this state of awareness, we no longer need to wear masks or assume various identities. We simply are, in harmony with the profound unity of existence. So, Amma's teachings reveal the intricate workings of ignorance, desire, and action in our lives. They offer a path to transcend this cycle by awareness of the present moment and recognizing our true nature. Through the lens of non-duality, we can shed the masks we wear, dissolve the illusion of separation, and experience the profound oneness that is at the heart of Amma's wisdom. The Upanishads inform us about our ever-free Self, but when there is an eclipse of ignorance, we become unaware of this Truth. That's where Mahatmas like Amma become torchbearers to the way of life and awaken us to living as awareness.

The Illusion of Desire

The more we vocalize our wants and desires, the deeper the feeling of lack permeates our being. This perpetual cycle of desire and longing is a source of unending suffering. However, a profound understanding in a non-dual way reveals that there is no duality, no second entity separate from us. In this realization, desires cease to exist, for everything is encompassed in the wholeness of existence. To see this clearly is to understand that there is no room for desire in the awareness of non-duality.

In the absence of separation, there is no craving to obtain something that is already an integral part of our being. Liberation from the idea of limitation occurs as soon as we recognize our true nature, unbounded and unlimited. It is the desire for freedom that breaks the shackles of limitations. The quest for happiness itself arises from ignorance, an ignorance of our innate essence – the Self's bliss, which is unconditional and intrinsic in nature. This innate essence embodies freedom, love, peace, and happiness. These qualities are not external constructs but are woven into the very fabric of our existence. They are absolute realities within Brahman. The Self, or Atma, is inherently Satchitananda – being, knowing, and bliss absolute.

If we truly understand this, then why do we experience a sense of incompleteness that drives us to seek happiness through relationships, wealth, fame, and recognition? Is it not a reflection of our desire to conform to societal norms and validate our humanity? This pursuit stems from ignorance about our own nature and the nature of all things as Satchitananda. This ignorance is the root cause of our struggles and failures. We relentlessly chase external sources of happiness and freedom, only to discover that it comes at a great cost, often leading to a lifetime of dissatisfaction and, ultimately, the inevitable call of mortality. There is no need to wait indefinitely, leading a miserable life and facing death with regrets. The wisdom passed down through the Guru Parampara, the lineage of spiritual teachers, echoes the profound revelation of "Tat twam asi" – "That Brahman you are."

This teaching awakens aspirants to their true nature, which is unconditional freedom and wholeness. It dismantles the illusion that we are limited individuals entangled in the complexities of the body and mind, endlessly pursuing happiness that remains elusive. Feelings, sensations, perceptions, and thoughts are mere misnomers, products of the indescribable illusion called Anirvachaneya Maya. This illusion deceives us into believing that we are limited entities, prompting us to endlessly search for happiness outside ourselves.

However, Sruti Guru points us toward our unchanging nature, declaring that we are Brahman – the absolute reality consisting of Sat (existence), Chit (consciousness), and Ananda (bliss), which is intrinsic to all things. It is ever-present, pure, conscious, and the ever-free Self. The illusion of desire and the pursuit of external happiness are rooted in ignorance of our true nature. The wisdom of the Guru Parampara, encapsulated in "Tat twam asi," reminds us of our innate wholeness and freedom. It dispels the illusion of limitation, guiding us toward self-realization and the recognition of our inherent Satchitananda nature, which transcends the endless pursuit of happiness in the external world.

The Quest for Immortality

Ignorance stands as the root cause of our struggles and failures. In our relentless pursuit of external sources of happiness and freedom, we often find ourselves paying a heavy price. This pursuit frequently leads to a lifetime marked by dissatisfaction, ultimately culminating in the inescapable call of Death. However, there is no need to resign ourselves to a lifetime of misery and regrets. The desire to depart peacefully from this world is a shared aspiration, leading us to seek the knowledge of immortality. The motto "Live peacefully to die peacefully" encapsulates this quest for a peaceful transition. This pursuit drives us to seek knowledge that transcends the limitations of the body-mind-world complex.

In this journey, Sruti, implores us to know "who am I," prompting us to contemplate what perishes and what endures. As individuals, we often perceive ourselves as isolated islands, each encircled by the walls of our body-mind complexes. We yearn to bridge these divides through relationships, but our lack of understanding frequently results in conflicts and wars, a reality that is all too evident today. These territorial divisions only serve to deepen our sense of limitation, perpetuating a cycle of misery.

The ancient Rishis, Guru Parampara imparted the wisdom of immortality. They did not view immortality from the perspective of the body-mind-world complex but from the standpoint of Atma, the Self. This perspective is eloquently conveyed in the teaching "Tat twam asi"—"That thou art." When we become aware of Atma as the absolute reality, we shed the misconception of being limited individuals confined to the roles of "doer" and "enjoyer." Through this understanding, it becomes clear that Satchitananda – existence, consciousness, and bliss – is the ultimate truth, while everything else is mere appearance born of ignorance. In the light of this realization, all transient aspects of existence are negated and sublated. The immortal Self transcends the cycle of birth and death, dispelling any room for misconception, misapprehension, or non apprehension. With this knowledge, we approach self-realization, recognizing the essence of our true nature. So, the quest for immortality is a journey from ignorance to self-realization. Ignorance is the root cause of our struggles and suffering as we chase external sources of happiness. However, through the Guru Parampara guides us to see immortality not as a facet of the body-mind-world complex but as a reality of the eternal Self. This understanding liberates us from the limited notion of individuality and leads us toward a state of enduring peace and self-awareness.

Wars

Wars, manifestations of humanity's darkest impulses, stem from the illusion of a separate self, akin to the delusion of a wave believing itself distinct from the ocean. In this erroneous perception lies the seed of conflict, as individuals and nations, consumed by the illusion of separateness, engage in ruthless pursuits of power, dominance, and control.

Just as the wave, oblivious to its intrinsic connection to the vast expanse of water, acts out of fear and insecurity, so too do warring factions operate from a place of ignorance and ego. Driven by greed, hatred, and the relentless pursuit of self-interest, they plunder the earth's resources, perpetrate atrocities, and sow discord and suffering in their wake.

Yet, like the wave crashing against the shore, their actions ultimately lead to their own destruction. As they wreak havoc upon the world, they sow the seeds of their own demise, blinded by the illusion of separateness and ignorant of the interconnectedness of all life.

It is only by transcending this illusion, by recognizing the fundamental unity that underpins existence, that humanity can hope to overcome the scourge of war. When individuals awaken to their inherent interconnectedness, when they realize that they are but expressions of the same divine essence, the impulse to harm and dominate diminishes, replaced by compassion, empathy, and a deep sense of belonging.

Thus, the path to peace lies not in the pursuit of power or the domination of others but in the recognition of our shared humanity and the embrace of our interconnectedness. Only then can wars cease, and humanity, united in purpose and vision, usher in an era of harmony, cooperation, and mutual flourishing.

Bridging the Gap Between Ideals and Realities

Wars often arise as a last resort when negotiations fail and threats to national security loom large. In the realm of geopolitics, conflicts over borders and territorial integrity can escalate rapidly, driven by the imperative to uphold constitutional rights and ensure justice under the law. When nations face external threats, whether from terrorist attacks or illegal incursions, the imperative to protect citizens and uphold the rule of law becomes paramount.

Indeed, the quest for peace is enshrined in the constitution of every nation, reflecting a commitment to safeguarding the well-being and rights of its people. In this context, the defense of borders and the enforcement of laws are not merely acts of aggression but essential measures to uphold national integrity and protect the sanctity of legal norms.

Morality, both individual and collective, lies at the heart of national identity and governance. A nation's duty to its citizens compels it to take stringent measures to ensure their safety and security, even if it means resorting to warfare as a means of defense. In the face of external threats, the enforcement of laws and the punishment of transgressors become indispensable tools for maintaining order and preserving social cohesion.

Moreover, the principles of international law and justice serve as guiding beacons in the pursuit of peace and stability on a global scale. Nations must respect the sovereignty of others and adhere to established norms of conduct, lest they invite condemnation and sanctions from the international community. In this interconnected world, where the rights of all humanity are sacrosanct, mutual respect and coexistence are essential for fostering harmony and understanding among nations.

Ultimately, while spiritual beliefs may inform individual actions and attitudes, the realm of national security and governance operates within the framework of constitutional principles and legal obligations. In matters of war and peace, the imperative to protect citizens and uphold justice transcends personal beliefs, serving as a cornerstone of national unity and cohesion. Through adherence to the rule of law and respect for international norms, nations can strive to create a world where the rights of all are upheld, and the pursuit of peace is a collective endeavor.

How Do We Help People During Wartime?

In the absence of the illusion of a separate self, our capacity for empathy expands boundlessly. We are moved to aid those in need, offering assistance in myriad ways, from providing shelter and financial support to offering solace and healing for their physical and emotional wounds. We become beacons of hope, assuring them that even in the darkest of times, there is light on the horizon.

Compassion extends even to those who perpetrate destruction, for they, too, are caught in the web of delusion. Unaware of the consequences of their actions, they unwittingly sow seeds of suffering for themselves and others. Rather than meet aggression with resistance, we respond with understanding, knowing that resistance only deepens their anguish.

In maintaining equanimity, we embody the perspective of the infinite. The Bhagavad Gita na dveshti na kankshati (12:17 verse) teaches us to transcend anger and desire, recognizing them as mere manifestations of the ego-bound mind. In embracing the fullness of being, we transcend the duality of perpetrator and victim, justice and injustice. Instead, we act from a place of pure compassion, where every action is imbued with healing intent.

In the realm of the infinite, there is no room for individual perspective or illusion. We act not from a sense of personal gain or righteousness but from a deep wellspring of compassion that knows no bounds. It is through this lens of boundless love that true healing and transformation occur, transcending the limitations of the ego-bound mind and ushering in a world of unity, peace, and wholeness.

In the realm of national security, spiritual principles can inform strategies that prioritize dialogue, diplomacy, and conflict resolution over aggression and violence. By seeking to understand the root causes of conflict and addressing them through peaceful means, nations can build lasting peace and stability.

Additionally, spiritual insights emphasize the unity of all life and the importance of environmental stewardship. National imperatives should include measures to protect the planet and promote sustainable development, recognizing that the well-being of future generations depends on the actions we take today.

Ultimately, harmonizing spiritual insights with national imperatives requires a shift in consciousness—one that transcends narrow self-interest and embraces the common good of humanity as a whole. By integrating these insights into governance and policy-making, nations can create a more just, peaceful, and sustainable world for all.

Love

"If you love Amma, you should love and serve all living beings. Only then can it be said that you love Amma. See everything as your own Self."

–Amma

Love expresses in its entirety because it is complete. There is no variation like the Sun. The Sun has no degrees of heat. The Sun does not say, 'Morning I will provide less heat, perhaps afternoon -more heat, by evening again little less heat, and by night I will not provide any heat. Changes in heat during the day are only superimpositions. In Reality, the Sun is free of all superimpositions.

Similarly, there is no anger or degrees of Love from a completeness standpoint. Love is expressed in its entirety.

But one says, 'I will love some, perhaps near ones like my family. I give more Love when coming to others again. But, love is given only a little, and I will not love other countries.' So, Love seems to change during favorable and unfavorable situations. But, these variations with dear ones or others are only superimpositions on the Self. Because of wholeness, in Reality, the Self is free of all superimpositions.

Therefore, everything and everyone is equally complete in nature, and being helped. Compassion has no limitations as it is infinite in nature. There is no hatred or attachment; that is real freedom.

The Guru is always silent and at peace. In that PRESENCE and silence, which is compassion, we get drawn and drown in the peaceful BEING when we go for Darshan.

Through silent conversation, the GURU reveals to us the quintessence of Truth that we are not a separate self but wholeness. So, there is no need to entail any form of belief as it is a direct experience. Moreover, that PRESENCE refers to the most inseparable and innermost aspect of everyone's experience.

Therefore, feeling that 'PRESENCE of GURU' is entirely available to all.

'GURU' means absolute PRESENCE. Thus, to revel in that timelessness in all mundane and spiritual actions is grace. However, that PRESENCE is a rare blessing. Thus, all our activities from mental level to physical level remain ever in peace, tranquility. Therefore they are available with total contentment and pure awareness. That's where all search for peace and happiness ends in GURU.

"To say 'I am love' brings fear to the ego because it threatens its existence. The separate ego-self fears the Truth, so it seeks to declare 'I love you' to gobble up and own anything or anyone it believes to be an object of happiness. Yet, everyone recognizes the unconditional Love and acceptance of 'Knowing-Being' during their daily experience of the deep sleep state. To recognize and live this Truth during the waking state is deliverance."

vidyā-vinaya-sampanne brāhmaṇe gavi hastini
śhuni chaiva śhva-pāke cha paṇḍitāḥ sama-darśhinaḥ

With the eyes of divine knowledge, the truly learned
see a learned and gentle brahmana, a cow, an
elephant, a dog, and a dog-eater with equal vision.
Bhagavad Gita Verse 5:18

Conflicts between individuals, families, or communities arise based on the belief that we are separate from each other. However, we share the same 'being, 'the wholeness.' So, division as a family cannot separate from the rest of humanity. That is why plants, animals, inert objects, and everything shares the same 'being.'

Suppose we want to make a real contribution to humanity; the most important thing is to be free from the belief that 'I am separate and others are separate.' So recognizing 'the isness,' whom everyone shares as their very 'beingness,' is essential because it is one, undivided life as a whole. So we should no longer have illusions , irrespective of whether people in our family like or dislike, agree or disagree. Therefore attending to a family or community can be done without the illusion of separateness. All mutual greetings take place in that wholeness.

Wars or peace are seen from the oneness of the 'being' standpoint. So all actions take place from that standpoint without preference towards anyone or anything. So there is no more illusion of attachment and aversion, which is a wholeness standpoint.

The enlightened ones possessed of humility see everything in this universe as Brahman itself without having 'neither desire nor aversion.' They just live as Awareness, the impartial witness of all.

9. Unconditional Freedom

"My children, The world is not the problem. The problem lies within the mind (the attention). The mind is the cause for your sorrows. So be watchful, and you will see things with greater clarity. Constant Watchfulness/Being Aware of Self (feeling of 'I') provides you with a penetrating eye and mind, so that you cannot be deceived. It will slowly take you closer to your true being: the bliss of the Self."

-Amma

Introduction

In existence, there exists an ineffable essence—an essence that eludes the grasp of language, defying the confines of our intellect and the limitations of our words. This essence is the embodiment of unconditional freedom, the very fabric of our being and the pulsating rhythm of all creation.

Yet, as we strive to comprehend the unfathomable, we find ourselves entangled in the intricate web of our own thoughts, our minds ceaselessly grasping for understanding, for meaning. And therein lies our plight—we yearn to encapsulate the essence of Amma, of existence itself, within the narrow confines of our intellect, hoping to confine the boundless within the finite.

But true liberation lies not in the confines of authority or doctrine, but in the fearless exploration of the unknown, in the silent contemplation of that which transcends comprehension. It beckons us to venture beyond the confines of our conditioned beliefs, to peer beyond the veil of the mind-body complex and the illusory world it conjures.

For the truth, the raw essence of existence, cannot be contained within the constructs of the mind. It defies categorization, eludes definition, and transcends the limitations of our conceptual frameworks. It simply is—beyond acceptance or denial, beyond the dichotomy of right and wrong, existing in a state of pure, unadulterated reality.

Let us then shed the shackles of our preconceptions, and instead, embrace the truth as it unfolds before us—unfiltered, unblemished, and unbound by the constraints of our understanding. Let us gaze upon existence with eyes unclouded by judgment, and in doing so, come to know the essence of unconditional freedom—the essence of Amma, and the essence of our own selves.

> *"Submission and surrender to the Guru is the royal path to supreme freedom.*
> *Surrender is nothing but giving up our likes and dislikes. That is when our heart opens. The Guru's grace is always present, but we should grant ourselves our own grace. That is surrender. When we surrender, we grant ourselves our own grace. Human birth and the guidance of a living sadguru are the greatest good fortune a soul can ever achieve. Understanding this, we should continue our efforts without wasting any time. If we have the attitude of surrender towards the Guru, the Guru's grace will surely take us to the supreme goal. Our life will attain fulfillment."*

-Amma

In the sacred journey of our spiritual evolution, we embark upon the path of prayer, not merely as a ritual, but as a means to cleanse the temple of our minds. This purification is not a mere external ritual, but a profound quest for clarity—a clarity that unveils the eternal Truth, the essence of Brahman, the pure awareness that permeates all existence.

At the heart of our pursuit lies the recognition that Brahman is not a distant object of knowledge, but the very essence of our being, the substratum upon which the entire cosmos dances. It is the eternal flame that burns within us, the silent witness to the unfolding drama of life.

Guided by the wisdom of the ancient scriptures, we are reminded of the profound truth encapsulated in the timeless teaching, "Tat Twam Asi"—"You are That." Through contemplation and reflection, we slowly unravel the veil of ignorance that obscures our understanding, gradually acquainting ourselves with the radiant presence of Brahman, which is our very essence.

As we journey deeper into the realms of self-discovery, we begin to discern the illusion of identification with the body-mind complex—the transient cloak that we mistakenly believed to be our true nature. With each prayer, with each moment of reflection, we inch closer to the realization of our innate divinity, casting aside the illusions of the ego to merge with the boundless expanse of pure awareness.

In this sacred dance of self-negation, we relinquish the shackles of limitation, surrendering to the vastness of our true nature. And in this sublime surrender, we find liberation—a liberation that transcends the confines of time and space, ushering us into the eternal embrace of Brahman, the ever-present reality that pulsates within us and all around us.

"I remember one of Amma's answers to a woman during a Satsang who was complaining how hard it was for her to share Amma with others, etc. Amma replied that a Guru is subtle, like space, air, or water. So if we try to grab and hold a bunch of air or water tightly in our fists, we will not be able to hold anything. Rather, if we open our fists or hearts wide, the water (grace) will overflow our palm (heart)!

According to Amma, the essence of unconditional freedom, embodied in the Guru, is revealed as the ultimate Truth. Yet, in our perpetual quest to grasp and comprehend, we inadvertently confine the boundless within the narrow corridors of our understanding. We succumb to the illusion of limitation, embracing the transient veils of identity, beliefs, and concepts as if they were our true essence.

Ensnared by the web of our own creation, we become prisoners of our perceptions, shackled by the confines of our conditioned minds. We cloak ourselves in the garb of limitation, adorning the myriad masks of identity crafted by societal constructs and personal narratives. And in doing so, we unwittingly perpetuate the cycle of separation—dividing ourselves and the world around us into neat compartments defined by ideology, creed, and nationality.

Yet, amidst the cacophony of conflicting beliefs and divergent paths, the Guru stands as a beacon of unwavering light—a guiding force that transcends the limitations of individual identity. The Guru is not merely a person but a manifestation of the eternal Truth, a pointer to the boundless expanse of unconditional freedom that lies within and without.

It is through the Guru's grace that we are invited to shed the constraints of our conceptual prisons, to pierce through the veils of illusion that shroud our perception, and to behold the radiant truth of our inherent divinity. For the Guru, in essence, is the embodiment of unconditional love—the eternal flame that ignites the dormant spark of realization within our hearts.

In recognizing the Guru as the manifestation of unconditional freedom, we transcend the divisive boundaries of sectarianism and tribalism, embracing the universal essence that unites all of creation. And in this sacred recognition, we reclaim our birthright as sovereign beings—free from the shackles of limitation, and immersed in the boundless ocean of unconditional love and freedom.

One of Amma's messages: "The Guru's body is the portal to infinity. The Guru's presence is the fullness of supreme truth and supreme happiness. The Guru embodies self-sacrifice in its ultimate state. In the sacred presence of the Guru, those who approach with humility and surrender are guided along the path of realization, wherein the veil of illusion is lifted, and the eternal Truth is unveiled. The Guru, transcending the limitations of form and conditionality, serves as a conduit for the revelation of our true nature—an essence that is boundless, unconditioned, and free from the shackles of conceptualization.

As the seeker embarks upon the journey of self-inquiry, guided by the Guru's wisdom, they come to recognize the Self-nature as unconditional freedom—an essence that eludes the grasp of the conditioned mind. For the mind, with its incessant chatter of thoughts, sensations, and perceptions, is but a vessel of limitation—a construct born of duality and separation.

In the radiant presence of unconditional freedom, the ignorance of conceptualized conditions is dissolved, like dew evaporating under the warmth of the morning sun. The Guru, like space, air, and water, is subtle and all-pervading—untouched by the transient fluctuations of the mind's machinations.

In contemplating the nature of unconditional freedom, one comes to realize that it transcends the confines of the mind's constructs. It is akin to the boundless radiance of the Sun, whose effulgence knows no bounds and whose light permeates every corner of existence. It cannot be constrained by the limitations imposed by the mind's conceptualizations, for it is the very essence of boundless potentiality and infinite possibility.

Thus, in the presence of the Guru, the seeker is invited to transcend the limitations of the conditioned mind, to bask in the luminous glow of unconditional freedom, and to realize the eternal truth that lies beyond the veil of illusion. In this sacred communion, the seeker is liberated from the confines of ignorance, emerging into the radiant expanse of boundless consciousness—a consciousness that knows no bounds and is forever free.

> *"If you vigorously keep rubbing the dust in your eyes instead of removing it, your pain and irritation will only increase. Remove the dust, and you will be all right. Similarly, the mind is like dust in the eye: it is a foreign element. Learn to get rid of the mind. Only then will you achieve perfection, bliss, and happiness."*

> **~Amma**

So, the mind, with its incessant need to categorize and conceptualize, attempts to confine the ineffable essence of the Guru within the narrow confines of individual identity. Yet, in doing so, it fails to grasp the profound truth that the Guru transcends the limitations of form and individuality. The Guru, like the vast expanse of nature itself, is impersonal—an essence that defies the constraints of labels and definitions.

Consider, for a moment, the futile attempt to capture the essence of nature on a camera or a mobile phone. Can we truly encapsulate the majesty of a towering mountain, the serenity of a tranquil lake, or the delicate beauty of a blooming flower within the confines of a snapshot? Similarly, can we reduce the vastness of our own being to a mere selfie, proclaiming, "This is who I am"? To do so would be to diminish the infinite depth and complexity of our true nature—to confine ourselves to the narrow confines of a label or an image.

And yet, despite our inability to capture the essence of nature or the essence of our own being, we persist in our attempts to do so—to confine the boundless within the limited framework of our understanding. We cling to fragmented ideas and concepts of the Guru, as if they could ever encapsulate the entirety of that which is beyond comprehension.

The same holds true for our conceptions of God—a concept that has been mired in the quagmire of human interpretation and misunderstanding since time immemorial. Each individual clings to their own image, their own story, their own symbols, desperately attempting to justify their version of reality. And in doing so, we perpetuate division and conflict, rather than embracing the unity and interconnectedness of all existence.

In the end, the truth remains elusive—a shimmering mirage on the horizon, forever receding as we attempt to grasp it. And so, perhaps the greatest wisdom lies in recognizing the limitations of our understanding, and surrendering to the vast expanse of the unknown—to the boundless expanse of unconditional freedom that lies beyond the confines of our concepts and beliefs.

In the silent sanctuary of meditative awareness, the veils of illusion are gently lifted, revealing the Guru not as a mere individual, but as a radiant embodiment of boundless compassion and love. With arms outstretched, the Guru stands as a beacon of light in the darkness of ignorance, ever-ready to guide us along the path towards realization and liberation.

In the presence of the Guru, all preconceived notions fall away, like autumn leaves surrendering to the gentle embrace of the wind. We are invited to cast aside the shackles of our limited understanding, and to behold the truth with eyes unclouded by judgment or expectation.

For the Guru is not confined to the narrow confines of individual identity, but is instead a vessel of divine grace—a conduit through which the infinite wisdom of the universe flows. With every breath, with every heartbeat, the Guru beckons us to awaken from the slumber of ignorance, and to embrace the boundless expanse of our true nature.

And so, with discernment as our guide, we embark upon the journey of self-discovery, surrendering to the guidance of the Guru as we navigate the uncharted waters of realization. With each step, with each moment of clarity, we draw closer to the luminous truth that resides within us and all around us—an eternal flame that burns brightly, casting aside the shadows of illusion and revealing the radiant splendor of unconditional freedom.

Analysis

In the silent embrace of deep sleep, we are enveloped in the boundless expanse of unconditional freedom—an ocean of undivided Oneness where distinctions dissolve into the ether. Here, there is no trace of the self or the other, no boundaries to separate us from the infinite expanse of existence.

In this state of profound stillness, there is no medium through which experience can unfold. The tapestry of consciousness lies dormant, untouched by the fleeting dance of perception. And yet, in this apparent void, lies the seed of all creation—the primordial essence from which the waking world emerges.

As we awaken from the depths of slumber, we find ourselves immersed in the waking state—a realm where unconditional freedom expresses itself through the intricate tapestry of the body-mind-world complex. Every sensation, every thought, every experience is but a shimmering reflection of the boundless essence that lies at the heart of all existence.

And yet, in our relentless quest to grasp the ineffable, we inadvertently imprison ourselves within the confines of concepts and preconceived notions. We attempt to capture the unbridled essence of unconditional freedom within the narrow confines of conditioned thought, thus obscuring its radiant splendor with the veil of conditional understanding.

In truth, unconditional freedom transcends the limitations of the mind's constructs. It is the very essence of existence itself—a radiant flame that flickers within us and all around us, illuminating the path towards liberation. And so, let us cast aside the shackles of conditioned perception, and embrace the boundless expanse of unconditional freedom that awaits us beyond the confines of the mind.

When we embark on a journey through the majestic mountains or stand in awe before the vast expanse of the ocean, our minds instinctively reach for the lens of conceptualization, eager to capture the beauty before us. Yet, in our haste to label and categorize, we often overlook the raw, unfiltered reality that lies beyond our preconceptions.

In this way, we traverse through life ensnared in the intricate web of our own perceptions and judgments. We interact not with the world as it is, but with the distorted reflections of our own conceptual frameworks. And in this dance of illusion, conflicts arise—dividing us into separate entities, each clinging to their own version of reality.

In our pursuit of freedom, we unwittingly surrender ourselves to the chains of conditioned thinking—submitting to the dictates of authority, religion, and ideology. We relinquish the boundless expanse of unconditional freedom in favor of the narrow confines of conditioned existence, trading the infinite for the finite in the name of security and certainty.

And so, we weave intricate narratives, crafting stories to justify our actions and beliefs, and enforcing them upon others through the muscles of power and influence. We cling to our ideologies with fervent zeal, willing to go to any lengths to protect them from perceived threats, even at the expense of individual freedom and autonomy.

Like the cow tethered to a long rope, we roam the pastures of life, grazing on the limited sustenance of conditioned existence. And yet, when the tether tightens, we find ourselves ensnared—bound by the limitations of our own making, unable to transcend the confines of our conditioned reality.

In this realization lies the invitation to break free from the chains of conditioned thinking, to cast aside the illusions of separation and division, and to embrace the boundless expanse of unconditional freedom that lies at the heart of all existence. It is only through this liberation of the mind and its construct that we can truly taste the sweetness of freedom, unencumbered by the limitations of our own making.

So, human existence, we find ourselves ensnared by the intricate web of concepts, symbols, and institutions that we ourselves have woven. From temples to churches, mosques to altars, we erect monuments to our interpretations of Truth, each proclaiming itself as the ultimate arbiter of reality.

Yet, in our fervent quest for certainty and security, we unwittingly bind ourselves to the chains of conditioned thinking, surrendering the boundless expanse of freedom in exchange for the comfort of familiarity. We cling to our beliefs with tenacious zeal, fearing the unknown and shunning any deviation from the prescribed path.

And so, we find ourselves caught in the grip of fear and guilt—emotions wielded like weapons by those who seek to maintain their hold on power and authority. We are made to feel small, insignificant, unworthy—told that our doubts and questions are signs of weakness, rather than the stirrings of a restless soul seeking truth.

In this state of emotional turmoil, we lose sight of reality—blinded by the veils of conditioned thinking and ensnared by the chains of our own making. We become prisoners of our own fears, unable to break free from the shackles of conformity and obedience.

But amidst the chaos and confusion, there remains a glimmer of hope—a spark of inner knowing that whispers of a reality beyond the confines of our conditioned existence. It is a call to transcendence, a beckoning towards the boundless expanse of unconditional freedom that lies dormant within us all.

In embracing this call, we reclaim our birthright as sovereign beings—free from the constraints of authority and dogma, liberated from the chains of fear and guilt. And in this sacred liberation, we discover the true essence of our being—the radiant light of truth that shines brightly, illuminating the path towards freedom and enlightenment.

We have woven a complex web of states, countries, and ideologies, each proclaiming itself as the epitome of freedom. Yet, in our relentless pursuit of these conceptual ideals, we inadvertently bind ourselves to the chains of conditioned thinking, sacrificing the boundless expanse of unconditional freedom for the illusion of security and control.

From the moment we are born, we are ensnared in a labyrinth of societal expectations and cultural norms—each thread binding us tighter to the fabric of our own limitations. We sacrifice our dreams, our aspirations, even our very lives, in service to these constructed ideals, believing that in doing so, we will find the elusive freedom we seek.

But in our blind devotion to these constructs, we become imprisoned within the confines of our own making. We build walls around ourselves and others, dividing humanity into tribes and factions, each vying for supremacy over the other. And in our desperation to protect our perceived freedoms, we only succeed in further entrenching ourselves in the cycle of bondage and separation.

Even our spiritual pursuits are not immune to this tendency to confine and control. We worship our gods and goddesses, each image and symbol a reflection of our own limited understanding. We take pride in our rituals and prayers, clinging to them like lifelines in a sea of uncertainty.

Yet, in our fixation on the forms, we lose sight of the formless—the boundless expanse of nature that lies beyond our concepts and constructs. We superimpose our frames of reference onto the world around us, limiting the infinite beauty and wonder of existence to mere words and symbols.

And so, like the silkworm weaving its cocoon, we find ourselves trapped within the confines of our own creation—unable to break free from the chains of conditioned thinking and experience the true freedom that lies beyond. It is only when we relinquish our attachments to these constructs, and surrender to the unbounded expanse of unconditional freedom, that we can truly experience the awe-inspiring majesty of life in all its unfiltered glory.

Recognition of Unconditional Freedom

In the profound journey of recognition, we embark upon a path of radical acceptance—an acceptance that transcends the limitations of labels, images, and hierarchical concepts that we impose upon ourselves and the world around us. It is a sacred invitation to behold reality as it truly is, unfettered by the constraints of conditioned thinking and preconceived notions.

In this state of recognition, there is neither denial nor acceptance of authority or ideology. Instead, there is a deep knowing—a profound awareness that encompasses the totality of existence without judgment or distinction. It is a recognition of the inherent interconnectedness of all things—a recognition that we are but threads woven into the intricate tapestry of life itself.

Living as awareness, we surrender to the boundless expanse of unconditional freedom—a freedom that knows no bounds and is not contingent upon external conditions or circumstances. It is a liberation from the shackles of the ego, a transcendence of the illusion of separation that pervades our collective consciousness.

In this state of pure awareness, we come to realize that all expressions of existence are but manifestations of the same eternal truth—the truth of unconditional freedom. Whether it be the rustle of leaves in the wind, the laughter of a child, or the quiet stillness of the night, each moment is a sacred expression of the divine unfolding of life itself.

And so, in the luminous glow of recognition, we find ourselves immersed in the radiant splendor of reality—a reality that transcends the limitations of the mind and embraces the infinite potentiality of the present moment. It is a state of profound grace—a state of total surrender to the boundless expanse of unconditional freedom that lies at the heart of all existence.

In the profound depths of deep sleep, where the mind's chatter fades into silence, there exists only the pure essence of unconditional freedom—a boundless expanse of Oneness without a second. In this state of being-ness alone, the very fabric of existence pulsates with the radiant glow of undivided unity.

As we awaken from the slumber of sleep, we find ourselves immersed in the waking state—a realm where unconditional freedom finds expression through the medium of the body-mind-world complex. Without the shackles of conditioning, the boundless expanse of unconditional freedom takes on the myriad forms of the world, dancing in the symphony of names and forms.

Just as the Sun shines forth in its self-illuminating glory, unaffected by the passing of time or the changing of seasons, so too does unconditional freedom radiate its eternal light through the ever-shifting landscapes of thoughts, sensations, perceptions, and feelings. From the perspective of unconditional freedom, there are no limits or boundaries—only the infinite expanse of possibility and potentiality.

In recognizing this reality with clarity, we come to understand that unconditional freedom cannot be attained, for it is already and always present in every moment, ever immediate and direct in its nature. To seek to attain it is to fall into the trap of conditioning, to confine the boundless within the narrow confines of the mind's constructs.

And so, we are invited to release the chains of conditioning—to let go of the need to establish authority or control through acceptance or denial of external concepts, practices, or symbols. Instead, we are called to embrace the boundless expanse of unconditional freedom with open hearts and clear minds, surrendering to the infinite majesty of existence in all its unfathomable beauty and wonder.

In the boundless expanse of existence, the attempt to capture the ineffable beauty of phenomena, whether it be the vastness of the sky, the depth of the ocean, or the majesty of a mountain, is akin to grasping at fleeting shadows. For in the silence of immensity lies the essence of unconditional freedom—a force that defies categorization and transcends the limitations of the mind.

In the presence of Amma, we are reminded of this eternal truth—that unconditional freedom is not something to be grasped or attained, but rather something to be allowed and embraced with open hearts and minds. In her embrace, we experience the freshness, the love, and the profound silence that are the hallmarks of unconditional freedom itself.

Even in the depths of mystical experiences or states of samadhi, we find ourselves humbled by the vastness of unconditional freedom—an essence that eludes our attempts at comprehension and transcends the boundaries of birth and death. For in the realm of unconditional freedom, there are no limitations, no boundaries—only the infinite expanse of possibility and potentiality.

Amma, in her infinite wisdom and compassion, serves as a living embodiment of unconditional freedom—an expression of the divine essence that permeates all of creation. In her presence, we are reminded of the boundless expanse of our own being, and the infinite potentiality that lies within us all.

And so, we are invited to surrender to the flow of unconditional freedom—to allow it to permeate every aspect of our being and to guide us along the path of awakening. For in the embrace of unconditional freedom, we find true liberation—a liberation that transcends the limitations of the ego and brings us into alignment with the infinite wisdom of the cosmos.

In the eternal dance of existence, the Sun shines forth as a radiant symbol of unyielding effulgence—a reminder of the boundless expanse of unconditional freedom that permeates all of creation. From the first light of dawn to the fading glow of twilight, we witness the ever-changing manifestations of the Sun's brilliance, each moment a testament to its timeless nature.

And yet, amidst the shifting tides of day and night, there lies a deeper truth—a truth that transcends the temporal ebb and flow of existence. It is the recognition that the Sun's effulgence is not bound by the constraints of time or circumstance, but is instead a manifestation of the eternal essence of unconditional freedom itself.

In the depths of deep sleep, where the mind's chatter fades into silence, we come face to face with this unbroken unity—an undivided Oneness that lies at the heart of all existence. Here, in the pure being-ness of the present moment, we experience the unblemished radiance of unconditional freedom in its purest form.

As we awaken to the waking state, it may seem as though unconditional freedom becomes obscured by the medium of the body-mind complex, lost amidst the myriad distractions and diversions of daily life. Yet, even in the midst of this apparent conditioning, the essence of unconditional freedom remains unchanged—like the Sun shining through a tiny hole in a darkened room, its brilliance undiminished by the shadows that surround it.

In the realm of knowledge, as in the realm of Awareness and inertness, unconditional freedom manifests in myriad forms, each a unique expression of the eternal truth that lies at the heart of all existence. And though the dance of birth and death may play out upon the stage of creation, the essence of unconditional freedom remains unblemished, immutable, and free from the constraints of time and space.

In recognizing this eternal truth with clarity and discernment, we come to know that unconditional freedom is not something to be attained or acquired, but rather something to be allowed and embraced with open hearts and minds. It is the very essence of our being—the radiant light that shines forth from the depths of our own souls, illuminating the path towards liberation and enlightenment.

So, existence, the essence of unconditional freedom dances gracefully, weaving through the tapestry of love, beauty, wholeness, and eternity. It is a dance of boundless joy and endless possibility—a dance that knows no limits or conditions, but flows effortlessly through the fabric of reality.

In the embrace of unconditional freedom, all play unfolds without constraint or restriction. From the fluttering of a butterfly's wings to the grandeur of a mountain peak, every moment is a divine expression of the eternal truth that lies at the heart of all creation.

And yet, try as we might, the mind and intellect falter in their attempts to grasp the essence of unconditional freedom. Beyond the realm of conceptualization lies a vast expanse of pure being-ness—a realm where the mind's chatter fades into silence, and only the Is-ness of Oneness remains.

In this state of deep sleep, where the mind and intellect are absent, unconditional freedom cannot be confined to the limitations of thought or understanding. It is a state of pure awareness—a recognition that no medium can condition or confine the boundless essence of existence.

Just as a wave cannot be separated from the ocean, so too is unconditional freedom inseparable from the fabric of reality. It is the very essence of all gods and goddesses, yet it cannot be contained or limited by any single concept or belief.

In recognizing the futility of rigid religious dogma or sectarian creeds, we come to understand that the ultimate Truth transcends the limitations of any one ideology or belief system. Instead, it is found in the recognition that all concepts, to a certain extent, point towards the same eternal truth—that of unconditional freedom.

And so, we are invited to allow the dance of unconditional freedom to flow through us—to surrender to its boundless beauty and infinite wisdom, and to embrace the truth of our own divine nature. The recognition of unconditional freedom is the true liberation and enlightenment—a liberation that transcends the limitations of the mind and brings us into alignment with the infinite expanse of existence itself.

So, all concepts, beliefs, and ideologies serve as threads that weave together the fabric of reality, each expressing a fragment of the eternal Truth—that of unconditional freedom. This Truth transcends the bounds of manifest and unmanifest, stretching beyond the limitations of time and space.

Unconditional freedom knows no bias or prejudice; it embraces all of existence in its entirety, manifesting in the dance of life in all its myriad forms. Yet, when we fail to recognize the Truth of unconditional freedom, we become ensnared in the web of our own concepts and perceptions, mistaking the shadows on the cave wall for reality.

Love, hate, pleasure, pain—all are but reflections of the conditioned mind, projections of our own desires and fears onto the world around us. We chain ourselves to the shackles of our own making, caught in the endless cycle of action and reaction dictated by the ego's narrow perspective.

But are we truly seeing each other? Are we truly hearing the whispers of the universe? In our relentless pursuit of division and distinction, we lose sight of the underlying Oneness that binds us all together—a Oneness that transcends the confines of our limited concepts and egoic identifications.

Misidentification is the root cause of our suffering, for it blinds us to the boundless expanse of unconditional freedom that lies within and without. Yet, throughout history, countless souls have sought liberation from this self-imposed prison, each through their own unique path—be it the path of yogis, tantrics, bhaktas, or seekers of worldly freedom.

But alas, all attempts to break free from the chains of conditioning ultimately fall short, for the concepts and traditions that have bound us for ages are deeply ingrained in the collective psyche of humanity. And so, we continue to spin our wheels in pursuit of freedom, unaware that the key lies in breaking free from our concepts, and in recognizing the Truth that lies beyond them—the Truth of unconditional freedom that is ever-present, ever-immutable, and ever-awaiting our recognition.

Conclusion

In the depths of deep sleep, where the mind's chatter fades into silence, we are bathed in the pure essence of unconditional freedom—an essence that transcends the limitations of names and forms, existing as a boundless expanse of pure being-ness. Here, in the stillness of the night, we are reminded that unconditional freedom is not something to be grasped or attained, but rather something to be allowed and embraced with open hearts and minds.

As we awaken to the waking state, the dance of unconditional freedom continues, flowing effortlessly through the myriad expressions of life in all its diversity. From the gentle rustle of leaves in the wind to the majestic roar of a waterfall, every moment is a divine expression of the eternal truth that lies at the heart of all existence.

Yet, amidst the ebb and flow of pleasure and pain, joy and sorrow, we often lose sight of the underlying Oneness that binds us all together. We become ensnared in the web of our own conditioning, reacting to the world around us based on our likes and dislikes, desires and fears.

But in reality, all experiences—whether pleasant or unpleasant—are but fleeting appearances on the canvas of existence, leaving behind impressions that shape our conditioned responses. Like the passing of an eclipse, they have no bearing on the eternal nature of unconditional freedom, which remains unchanged and unaffected by the transient fluctuations of the world.

In recognizing this eternal truth with clarity and discernment, we come to understand that ourselves and everything around us are manifestations of the same divine essence—that of unconditional freedom. And it is through the process of hearing, reflecting, and meditating on these truths that we come to realize our inherent connection to the boundless expanse of existence, and find liberation in the embrace of unconditional freedom.

It's akin to the dance of a river merging with the vast expanse of the ocean.

Picture this: the river, a flowing stream of water, and the ocean, an endless body of water. Yet, when they unite, distinctions vanish as water becomes one, boundless and eternal.

These descriptions, though profound, are mere attempts to capture the ineffable. Reality transcends these conceptual confines.

In the same vein, the individual, immersed in hearing and contemplation, embodies inherent freedom, yet often remains unaware of this profound truth. Through meditation and discernment, one peels away the layers of illusion to unveil the essence of unconditional freedom.

As the realization dawns, the illusory boundaries of individuality dissolve, revealing the timeless unity that underpins all existence. Names and distinctions fade into insignificance in the radiant light of this eternal Oneness.

Thus, terms like realization and enlightenment are but feeble expressions of the boundless expanse of unconditional freedom. In truth, it transcends all concepts, for it is not merely a concept but the very essence of existence itself.

Consider the analogy of visiting a shoe shop: the shopkeeper presents a shoe, but it doesn't quite fit. Instead of exploring other sizes, attempting to squeeze into the same shoe size would be futile. It's akin to reshaping one's foot to match the shoe—a notion that's impractical and, frankly, absurd. Similarly, in our quest for truth, we often try to conform to various authorities, doctrines, and ideologies, hoping to find the perfect fit. Yet, in doing so, we sacrifice our inherent freedom, trading it for the illusion of certainty and security.

Amma's wisdom cuts through this illusion, reminding us that clinging to concepts is akin to surrendering our freedom for mere trinkets. We're not meant to blindly accept or reject any concept, whether self-imposed or imposed by others. Instead, we're called to simply observe the truth as it unfolds—naked, unadorned, and unaltered.

Let us offer these reflections on unconditional freedom at the divine feet of Amma, the embodiment of boundless love and wisdom, who guides us to the realization of our innate freedom.

> *"May the Guru within all my children awaken. May my children discover this Guru within. The mirror to remove all your impurities is within you, my children. Look into it, remove your impurities and become mirrors yourselves. May all my children be happy. May divine grace bless my children."*

> **-Amma**

Appendix

Letter to Satsang Group on New Year 2024

The arrival of a new year often marks a time of reflection, renewal, and setting intentions for the future. It provides us with an opportunity to assess our lives, our actions, and our goals. It's a time when many people make resolutions to improve themselves or their circumstances. However, beyond the typical resolutions, there is a deeper and more profound theme that can guide us in the coming year – that theme is "living in Awareness." This concept emphasizes the importance of recognizing Truth, consciousness, and bringing that light of Self-realization into every aspect of our lives. In the following discussion, let us explore why living in Awareness is such a meaningful theme for the New Year and how it can positively impact our journey ahead, from the standpoint of wisdom imparted by ancient rishis. Living in Awareness is an attitude that encompasses our mind, thoughts, words, and actions as situations unfold in our lives. It involves recognizing the state of Being-ness and Awareness by acknowledging it, as mentioned in Drg-drsya viveka – "asti bhAti priyaM" in verse 1.

This Awareness should be present in whatever we do, rather than going through life on autopilot. The first 'asti' is the basic essence, Being, the adhishtanam, the foundation of all experience. The moment we speak of existence, then automatically the consciousness, the Knowing, is present. That is the 'bhaathi'. Without being 'conscious' of a thing, we cannot speak of its existence. The above two aspects are the 'Sat and Chit.' The third, 'priyam,' the 'Ananda,' in other words, the exclusiveness of Being-Knowing, is Bliss absolute. The love that one possesses towards one's own Self is due to this aspect of Truth.

Amma says just as anytime one enters a river, for whatever purpose such as taking a bath or offering prayers, we know that they will return. No one seeks to get lost in the river. In the same way, apart from one's education to earn a livelihood, one must learn that in life itself, we ultimately return to the Self. This mindfulness is the key to our life. Similarly, when we are handling fragile things that may break, we are careful. Again, when dealing with fire, water, electricity, or engaging in dangerous acts, all our attention and focus come to the forefront, and our reflexes play a vital role in avoiding accidents. So, mindfulness is important in worldly life and spiritual realization. When one seeks to return to the Self, we get all the help necessary. The Guru and Sruti (Upanishads) help us recognize the Self.

It's always the teaching of Lord Krishna in the Bhagavad Gita (2:14) that all things should be seen according to their nature because they arise in time and dissipate in time. Happiness and misery are the same in this regard, so we should be alert, aware, and awake to the timeless Truth that they do not have permanence. It's our mind that builds castles in the air and seeks permanence in this world.

The entire creation is in flux, so we cannot find a permanent state to settle in, as it would go against the nature of things. We cannot go against nature but must become aware and navigate our lives by imbibing the truth of what is Sat, the essence, Being, Existence, and what is not. By surrendering to Ishwara, the Omniscient God who has fabricated the creation out of Sat and not Asat, (Bhagavad Gita 2:16) we understand that Being-Knowing is the essence in all, like gold in ornaments.

According to the nature of things, we can act, talk, and think in our day-to-day activities while interacting with people and things that require our involvement. All prayers, as Amma says, are not for Ishwara to hear; rather, we ourselves should hear and become aware, giving space to non-violence, peace, and moral values that we expect from others, and we should implement the same towards others.

Amma says that all our religious practices should not cause harm, and we should respect each other with understanding.

"Years pass, and years arrive, signifying the passage of time. Within this ever-changing temporal existence, there is a constant and unchanging essence represented by the "I." This essence is not created or defined by external factors but radiates like a fragrance from within.the Upanishads, ancient Indian scriptures, proclaim that our true nature, "I," known as Pratyagatma (the inner Self), is also Sarvatma (the Self of all). It is characterized by Ananyatwam, indicating inseparability and oneness without a second. In simpler terms, it means that our inner Self is the same in essence as the universal Self that pervades all of existence. Furthermore, the Upanishads emphasize that every thought, sensation, perception, and feeling we experience is an effulgence or manifestation of this inner Self, "I," which is both the source of consciousness and the knower of all experiences, Sat-Chit, when we vocalize as "I exist."

The scriptures emphasize that knowing and realizing this Self is of paramount importance, as it is more precious than anything else, even dearer than a son. The realization is described in Br Up 1-4-10 as a state where the Self knows only Itself as "I am Brahman," and as a result, it becomes everything in existence. The teachings also caution against the erroneous belief that anything is separate from the Self "I," as it alone is the singular experience of all, direct and immediate, but easily mistaken as the body-mind-world complex. True understanding recognizes the unity of the Self, and any perception of separateness is based on superficial attributes such as name, form, and actions. The Upanishadic teachings encourage us to recognize and meditate upon our inner Self as the ultimate Truth, realize its oneness with the universal Self, and transcend the limitations of external appearances and distinctions. This understanding leads to a deeper awareness and a profound shift in our perspective on life.

The Brihadaranyaka Upanishad (2-4-5) emphasizes that the Self should be realized as it alone is worthy of realization or should be made the object of realization. Our love for other objects is secondary because they contribute to the pleasure of the individual self or ego, and our love for the Self alone is primary. As Amma says, realization should be 'I am Love,' and to realize this, Self-knowledge is needed. This realization process involves hearing about the Self, reflection on the Self, and meditation on the Self. The Chandogya Upanishad (6-14-2) states, "ācāryavān puruṣo veda," which means "a person who has a teacher acquires Self knowledge." Therefore, we should hear about the Self from a teacher and through the scriptures.

The realization of the "I" Self occurs through a process of hearing, reflection, awareness, and meditation, leading to a deep conviction. Therefore, the practice of religion is not limited to visiting temples but also involves understanding the principles behind them. Temples and their symbols and attributes of Ishwara serve as aids to help individuals come back to the Self.

The creation and the creator are considered one from Brahman, the absolute standpoint which alone is Atma, the Self of all. It is essential to sit with the desire to meditate. Especially when worldly desires are strong and are pulling us into the world of Nama (names) and Rupa (forms). So, focus on Self "I," but in the right way, not keeping it confined to the body-mind-world complex. A focused mind and perseverance are necessary for progress in meditation. Understanding the impermanent nature of life is crucial. We should balance our spiritual and worldly lives, knowing that life is transient. Therefore, it is important to perform good deeds regardless of circumstances; good karma improves our lives. It's essential to focus on doing good in the present, as past lives have relevance. Dwelling on the past or worrying about the future is futile; instead, we should focus on the present moment, which helps us come to the Self by clearing our distractions. Thus, meditation is beneficial, leading to self-awareness. We are always meditating on outward objects, so now, with effort, we should strive to live in the present and engage in selfless service. Acts of kindness and compassion improve our meditation.

Discernment to return to the Self and make wise choices is essential. We should focus on our inner Self rather than external distractions. Surrendering to the divine through service is important. We should prioritize our actions and thoughts to cause no harm, as all these actions prevent us from coming back to Self.

We should prioritize meditation and spiritual practice over wasteful activities like excessive phone and TV use. Reading books and developing love and compassion can awaken our true selves. Ego and attachment are obstacles to spiritual growth. Power and material pursuits are illusions. We should focus on merit and virtue, bringing light into our lives and dispelling darkness. So all these teachings are pointers to come to Self.

Awareness should be directed upward, like fire rising. A focused mind is more potent than mere imitation. Learning from other cultures and practices can enrich our lives. Our minds should be still and silent, like a serene lake. Life is like an exam hall, and we should live without unnecessary tension, seeking the help of Ishwara. Praying to Ishwara and meditating on the Self can help bring our minds back to stillness and regulate our thoughts. We should rest in the present moment and meditate on our true nature "I." This is the wisdom that Amma imparts.

When we visit a friend's house and encounter their guard dog, we naturally call out to our friend to retrain it. In response, our friend takes the initiative to tie up the dog and safely leads us inside. Similarly, when we call upon Ishwara, the divine, with sincere devotion and seeking, Ishwara takes care of us. Ishwara not only created this universe but also governs it, through divine will. Just as a friend protects us from any harm posed by their dog, Ishwara safeguards us from the illusory and deceptive aspects of the world, known as Maya. Ishwara's protection and guidance help us navigate through the complexities and illusions of the material world. Through this divine intervention, we are led on a path of self-discovery and realization of the ultimate truth, the Atma, the Self, which is none other than Brahman, the universal consciousness that underlies all existence. Ishwara's grace and revelation guide us from the realm of Maya towards the profound understanding of our essential nature and of all existence. In essence, Ishwara plays a pivotal role in assisting us on our spiritual journey, just as a friend ensures our safety and comfort when we visit their home.

In conclusion, all conflicts and fights that arise in our lives take us away from our true Self. These disturbances have no lasting reality, much like a fleeting dream. Our anger and desires, although they may seem everlasting, are, in fact, short-lived. The Bhagavad Gita (2:14) 'Agamāpāyino anityā' reminds us that everything is impermanent.

As we enter this new year 2024, I pray that all of Amma's children develop the inner strength to let go of these fleeting disturbances, cultivate a true understanding of the Self and live as Awareness. This understanding allows us to reject the fleeting ego nature and the world, and to remain centered and aligned with the timeless Truth of our existence.

The Method and Benefits of Using Awareness and Visualization for Pain Management: Incorporating Self Recognition

Pain management through awareness and visualization not only leverages the mind's profound influence over the body but also invites a deeper exploration of the Self, which is inherently free from pain. This method, rooted in focused attention and imaginative healing, extends beyond mere symptom relief, guiding individuals towards a profound recognition of their true nature beyond body-mind identification.

How to Practice

Direct Awareness to the Pain: Initiate the practice by consciously directing your awareness to the area of pain, fully engaging with the sensation without judgment. Meditate on the area causing pain, bringing total awareness to it. Feel your healing touch within that region. Visualize creating a healing presence beneath the skin, running your hand directly over tissues, muscles, bones, arteries, veins, ligaments, and organs. This step is crucial for isolating the pain and preparing the mind for deeper work.

Engage in Healing Visualization: With awareness anchored in the painful area, visualize a healing force emanating from within, running your hand directly, soothing the afflicted tissues, muscles, bones, and organs. Imagine this healing energy as an extension of your awareness, capable of reaching and mending the deepest parts of your being.

Holistic Healing of Emotional Distress: Pain is often intertwined with emotional suffering. Through visualization, extend your healing touch to areas of emotional pain, allowing your awareness to dissolve these distresses, recognizing them as temporary and not intrinsic to your true nature.

Maintain Steady Awareness and Recognize the Self: Maintain unwavering awareness, whether with eyes closed or open. As you do this, the pain will gradually subside over seconds to minutes. Keep the awareness constant and continue the mental stroking of your hand over the area until the pain completely dissipates. During this process, begin to recognize that your essence, or Self, is perpetually free from the pain experienced by the body-mind. Keep your focus unwavering, and as you do, begin to recognize that your essence, or Self, is ever free from the pain experienced by the body-mind complex. Understand that pain, like a distorted image in a concave or convex mirror, is a misrepresentation affected by the condition of the mirror, not the reality of the image itself. Similarly, pain appears in the Self due to identification with the body and mind but is not an inherent attribute of the Self.

Benefits

Empowerment and Non-Pharmacological Relief: This practice empowers individuals by providing a non-invasive method to manage pain, free from the risks associated with pharmacological treatments.

Recognition of the Self's Freedom from Pain: A key benefit of this method is the recognition that the Self is inherently free from pain. This awareness brings a profound sense of peace and liberation, knowing that pain is a condition of the body-mind identification and not of the Self.

Holistic Approach to Well-being: By addressing both the physical and emotional aspects of pain and recognizing the true nature of the Self, this practice offers a holistic path to healing. It acknowledges the illusion of mind, body, with Self, aiming for a state of well-being that transcends physical symptoms.

Enhanced Mind-Body Connection: Regular practice fosters a deeper connection between the mind and body, enhancing awareness and sensitivity to bodily sensations. This awareness can lead to healthier lifestyle choices and a greater appreciation for the body's signals.

Stress and Anxiety Reduction: The calming effect of visualization and the recognition of the Self's freedom from pain contribute to reduced stress and anxiety levels, creating a positive feedback loop that further alleviates physical discomfort. Incorporating the recognition of the Self's inherent freedom from pain into the practice of awareness and visualization offers a transformative approach to pain management. It not only addresses the immediate experience of pain but also guides individuals towards a deeper understanding of their true nature, free from the transient afflictions of the body and mind. This comprehensive method not only promises relief from physical discomfort but also paves the way for lasting peace and liberation from the cycles of pain and identification with the body-mind complex.

"I" in Now - Presence

Introduction

"I in Now" embodies the essence that everything is all there is, revealing that the perceived separation between ourselves and the world is an illusion. In this perspective, past and future are mental constructs, while 'I,' the true Self, exists only in the eternal presence. By fully recognizing this presence, 'I' realize that the life unfolds here and now, dissolving the boundaries between the separate self and others. This understanding brings a profound sense of oneness, similar to the exclusivity experienced in deep sleep, highlighting that 'I' is not a separate entity moving through time and space but is the very presence itself—eternal, pure, conscious, and free - Nitya, Suddha, Buddha, Muktha—embodying wholeness.

'I' reveals the essence Self, or pure awareness, which is unconditioned and beyond time and space. "I In Now" reflects this timeless nature, where 'I' is not confined to the body or mind but is the Spurana, the spark, the effulgence, the awareness of Consciousness in which all experiences arise and dissolve. By recognizing this presence, 'I' is peace and contentment throughout. Thus, when the limitations of the ego—Ahamkara ('I' forms) taking the names and forms—dissolve, they resolve into the true Self as pure presence and awareness, freeing the sense of separation.

"I in Now" is the true Self, recognized as eternal presence, beyond the constructs of time and space. This understanding leads to a life of peace, contentment, and unity, where the illusion of separation fades away, revealing the inherent oneness of all existence. Through this awareness, 'I' remains as pure consciousness, embodying the timeless, free, and whole nature of the true Self.

Purpose of the 'True Nature' Device

Let us imagine a device exists whose purpose is to provide an instantaneous (or near-instantaneous) recognition of our True Nature, which is unconditional, whole, and free.

Unconditional: This recognition is not influenced by anything external. It transcends the changing conditions of our lives, revealing a state of being that is perpetually pure and untouched.

Whole: It unveils the completeness of our existence. Beyond the limitations of the physical body and the mind, it allows us to experience our true Self as infinite and indivisible.

Free: It liberates us from all constraints and bindings. In this state of awareness, we recognize that our true Self is boundless, unrestricted by the confines of time, space, or identity.

By providing this direct and immediate connection to our True Nature, this device serves as a beacon of clarity and liberation, enabling us to live every moment in the light of our eternal, blissful essence.

Bridging Ancient Wisdom with Modern Life

The Upanishads expound on our True Nature as Sat, Chit, Ananda—Existence, Consciousness, and Ever-Blissful—in an abstract format, save for some direct statements like the mahavakyas ("Tat Tvam Asi" - Thou art That). Through constant sravana (listening), manana (contemplation), and nidhidhyasana (conviction) of these scriptural texts, one gains a deep understanding and conviction that their true nature is indeed SatChitAnanda.

For those who have dedicated their lives to the study of scripture, such as sannyasins, it is a part of their routine to allocate large amounts of dedicated time for this purpose. However, the vast majority of people find it challenging to carve out such uninterrupted time due to work, constant interruptions from other duties like raising children, and the multitude of powerful distractions that fragment the focus of the mind.

Given that the realization of one's True Nature is described as instantaneous in the Upanishads, there is a compelling need for a tool that can facilitate this realization seamlessly amidst the chaos of modern life. Imagine a device, akin to a single-purpose cell phone, that can immediately remind us of our True Nature and shed the layers of misidentification, regardless of the situation.

This tool would be fundamentally different from existing practices such as mantra japa, which involves the repetition of sacred sounds to cultivate a particular mental state. Instead, this device would provide direct and immediate recognition of our non-dual nature. It would work effortlessly in any circumstance, whether we are experiencing bodily pain, emotional turbulence, or intellectual confusion.

Such a device would serve as a constant, unwavering reminder of our inherent essence, much like the mahavakyas do in their succinct brilliance. It would encapsulate the essence of the Upanishads, refined for contemporary use, offering a bridge between ancient wisdom and modern living. This True Nature Device would help us connect instantly with our SatChitAnanda essence, enabling us to live every moment in the light of our eternal, blissful Self, free from the distractions and interruptions of daily life.

By integrating this profound wisdom into a form that is both familiar and accessible, this tool would empower individuals to transcend the confines of misidentification and experience the boundless joy of their true nature, even amidst the busyness of modern life.

The Possibility of a True Nature Device

It is therefore likely that a tool can exist that immediately reminds one of one's True Nature and sheds misidentification in the midst of any activity. This remarkable device would serve as an ever-present guide, instantly connecting us to our inherent essence of freedom and bliss, transcending the limitations of traditional practices.

While some may argue that tools like Mantra Japa already exist to aid in this realization, we propose that this tool would be fundamentally different. Unlike mantra japa, which involves the replacement of one thought with another through repetition, this device would bypass such intermediary steps. It would directly and instantaneously allow the user to recognize their non-dual nature, unveiling the eternal presence that underlies all experiences.

Such a device would function seamlessly in any circumstance, be it during moments of bodily pain, emotional turbulence, or intellectual confusion. By reflecting our true Self, it would help us see beyond the illusions of separation and misidentification. This device would embody the essence of the Upanishads, refined for contemporary use, and would serve as a constant reminder of the unchanging, infinite, and unconditional nature of our true Self.

This possibility symbolizes a profound leap in spiritual practice, offering a tool that integrates the timeless wisdom of the Upanishads into a form that is both familiar and transformative. It would provide an immediate connection to our True Nature, guiding us to live every moment in the light of our eternal essence, free from the confines of misidentification.

The True Nature Device

Imagine a device, akin to a single-purpose cell phone, that connects you directly to your True Nature—an essence that is free and ever blissful. This extraordinary tool instantly removes the misidentification accumulated through life, bypassing the traditional methods of sravana (listening), manana (reflection), and nidhidhyasana (meditation).

This device functions flawlessly in any situation of misidentification, be it bodily pain, emotional turbulence, or intellectual misunderstanding. While it does not dissolve bodily or emotional pain directly, it enables the user to recognize their True Nature, helping them identify the necessary tools to rectify their issues. Like a mirror, it allows us to recognize ourselves while understanding that the mirror image is not separate from us. It ensures there is no prejudice or judgment of feelings and thoughts, although this is not its primary function.

It operates with the familiarity and simplicity of a dial phone, guiding us effortlessly to the realization that we are whole, infinite, and unconditional. Just as light takes the shape of objects but never loses its nature, this device reveals our True Nature in every circumstance. It embodies the inseparability of the sun and sunlight, and the essence of the wave that is nothing but water.

The Upanishads describe the moment we wake up as a profound realization of our True Nature. The first Sphurana (effulgence, spark) of awareness is our pure Self, before the mind begins to shape the world around us. This device captures that initial spark, connecting us to our True Nature immediately, regardless of external conditions. It serves as a metaphorical representation, reminding us of the ever-present connection to our deepest essence, echoing the timeless wisdom of the Upanishads.

While the Upanishads emphasize the necessity of direct realization and inner experience, they suggest that the True Nature is beyond any physical device, residing within the heart of each being. However, as a metaphorical representation, this device can serve as a powerful reminder and guiding tool to help individuals reconnect with their true Self, reflecting the timeless essence of the Upanishads in a way that resonates with modern life.

Thus, the True Nature Device, though not a physical object, symbolizes a tool of profound self-realization. It seamlessly integrates the wisdom of the Upanishads into a form that is familiar and accessible, helping us transcend misidentification and connect with our eternal, blissful essence in every moment of our lives.

Supporting the Wisdom of Sruti

The True Nature Device is not just a modern invention; it is deeply rooted in the ancient wisdom of the Upanishads. These sacred texts encapsulate the essence of our being, offering timeless truths that resonate with the purpose of this device.

In the beginning, dear one, this was Being, Existence, ISness alone, one without a second. This device mirrors this profound teaching by reminding us of our inherent oneness with the universe, transcending the illusion of separateness now as we read or hear these words.

–Chandogya Upanishad 6.2.1

That which is immediate, direct so, directly perceived as Brahman. This device embodies this truth by providing an immediate, direct experience of our True Nature, without the need for intermediary steps or prolonged practice.

Brihadaranyaka Upanishad 3.5.1

I am Brahman. This profound declaration is at the heart of the device's purpose. It serves as a constant reminder of our divinity, our intrinsic connection to the absolute reality.

Brihadaranyaka Upanishad 1.4.10

It is known in every state of consciousness. The device operates seamlessly in all situations—whether in moments of bodily pain, emotional turbulence, or intellectual confusion—allowing us to recognize our True Nature, which pervades all states of being.

Kena Upanishad 2.4

Metaphors from the Upanishads

The Upanishads offer profound metaphors to illustrate our True Nature:

Light and Objects: Just as light takes the shape of the objects it illuminates without losing its intrinsic nature, our True Nature remains ever-present and unchanging, regardless of the forms and experiences we encounter. The light is constant, pure, and unaffected by the shapes it reveals.

Sun and Sunlight: The sun and its sunlight are inseparable in nature. Similarly, our True Nature is an integral, indivisible part of our being. The essence of who we are is inherently connected to the divine source, much like sunlight emanates from and is one with the sun.

Wave and Water: A wave is nothing but water. It may rise and fall, taking various forms, but its essence remains unchanged. In the same way, our True Nature is like water—pure and constant—despite the ever-changing waves of our thoughts, emotions, and experiences. The wave is a manifestation of water, just as our individuality is a manifestation of the universal self.

These metaphors from the Upanishads beautifully convey the idea that, despite the myriad forms and experiences of life, our True Nature remains pure, whole, and free—unaffected and eternal.

Refining the Abstract Teachings of the Upanishads into a Single Purpose Tool

The Upanishads, with their profound and abstract teachings, guide us towards the realization of our True Nature—an essence that is boundless, blissful, and free. To distill these timeless insights into a single-purpose tool akin to an old dial phone, which provided a near-instantaneous connection between individuals, we must envision a device that can immediately connect us to our True Nature, regardless of the situation.

Imagine a device, simple yet powerful, that acts as an unerring bridge to our inner Self. Just as the old dial phone required no complex steps to establish a connection, this tool effortlessly aligns us with the essence of who we are. It transcends the need for gradual practices and mental conditioning, offering direct and immediate access to the ever-present truth within us.

It would not seek to replace thoughts with other thoughts, calm the mind for contemplation, or foster positive imaginations. Instead, it would mirror our true Self, reminding us of our inherent nature beyond thoughts, emotions, and sensations.

This tool would embody the distilled wisdom of the Upanishads, refined for contemporary use. By bypassing traditional methods and mental constructs, this device would offer a direct experience of our True Nature, serving as a beacon of clarity and liberation in any situation.

While the Upanishads emphasize the inner journey and personal realization, the concept of this tool serves as a metaphorical representation—a reminder of the ever-present connection to our deepest essence.

What the Device Is Not

1. Not a Mantra Japa Tool:

This device is not meant for mantra japa, which is the practice of replacing one thought with another through the repetition of sacred sounds or phrases. Unlike mantra japa, which engages the mind in focused repetition to cultivate a specific mental state, this device seeks to connect you directly to your True Nature without the intermediary of repetitive thought.

2. Not a Dhyana/Dharana Tool:

It is not a Dhyana or dharana tool, which aims to calm the thoughts of the mind and allow for deep contemplation. While Dhyana and dharana are practices that cultivate inner stillness and concentration, this device transcends the need for such mental techniques by facilitating an immediate recognition of your ever-present, blissful essence.

3. Not a Bhavana Tool:

This device is also not about bhavana, which involves positive imaginations that align the user with productive thoughts and feelings. Bhavana practices use the power of positive visualization to transform the mind and emotions. In contrast, this device bypasses the realm of imagination, guiding you straight to the realization of your true, unconditioned Self.

By understanding what this device is not, we can appreciate its unique purpose: to serve as an immediate conduit to our True Nature, free from the traditional methods of mental engagement, contemplation, and imagination.

The True Nature Device

Immediate connection to True Nature
Universal Unconditionality in All Circumstances
Essence of the Upanishads
Familiar and Intuitive Interface

Can such a device exist?

However, as a metaphorical representation, this device can serve as a powerful reminder and guiding tool to help individuals reconnect with their true Self, reflecting the timeless essence of the Upanishads in a way that resonates with modern life.

Thus, the True Nature Device, though not a physical object, symbolizes a tool of profound self-realization. It seamlessly integrates the wisdom of the Upanishads into a form that is familiar and accessible, helping us transcend misidentification and connect with our eternal, blissful essence in every moment of our lives.

Thus, our essence remains pure, whole, and free, regardless of the forms we take or the experiences we undergo. "Aham asmi" — I exist. This existence is not bound by the transient and the changing. Just as light remains untainted by the forms it illuminates, and as the wave remains water despite its shape, our true Self remains untouched by the ephemeral. We are the eternal essence, pure and unbroken. In every breath, in every moment, let us remember this profound truth. We are not merely the sum of our experiences or the roles we play. At our core, we are the undying light, the eternal presence, the very essence of being. Thus, we are now going into device — Aham asmi. I exist, and in this existence, I am whole.

"Aham asmi" (I exist)

This simple yet profound statement encapsulates the essence of our being. It signifies the fundamental truth of one's own existence and the inherent state of being that pervades every moment of consciousness. The True Nature Device is a constant reminder of this ever-present reality, reinforcing the recognition of our unchanging, eternal essence.

In the vast expanse of reality, amidst the ceaseless flux of thoughts, sensations, and perceptions, there exists a profound truth that transcends the ephemeral nature of existence. This truth is encapsulated in the simple yet profound statement: "I exist." Within these two words lie the essence of being, the heartbeat of consciousness, and the eternal substratum underlying all experiences.

At its core, "I exist" signifies the fundamental truth of one's own existence. It is a declaration of self-awareness, a recognition of the inherent state of being that pervades every moment of consciousness. In uttering these words, one acknowledges their presence in the world, affirming their place in the essence of existence.

However, the significance of "I exist" extends far beyond mere acknowledgment of individual existence. It serves as a gateway to deeper realms of understanding, inviting contemplation on the nature of reality itself.

Indeed, "I exist" is not confined to the realm of personal identity but resonates with the very fabric of reality. It is the pulse of the universe, the heartbeat of existence itself. Just as every wave is an expression of the ocean, every individual existence is a manifestation of the underlying Absolute consciousness.

In the state of deep sleep, where the chatter of the mind subsides and the boundaries of the self dissolve, "I exist" shines forth in its purest form. It is the exclusive essence of existence, devoid of the complexities of the waking world. In this state, one merges with the eternal flow of consciousness, experiencing a profound sense of unity with all that is.

Moreover, "I exist" embodies not only the state of being but also the state of bliss. Beyond the fluctuations of pleasure and pain, joy and sorrow, lies a deeper, unconditional happiness that arises from the realization of one's true nature. This bliss is not dependent on external circumstances but is inherent in the very core of existence.

The profound wisdom encapsulated in "I exist" is echoed in the ancient teachings of Vedanta, which proclaim the identity of the individual self (Atman) with the intrinsic consciousness, Brahman, the absolute reality. The famous declaration "Tat Tvam Asi" – "Thou art That" – encapsulates this truth, affirming the essential unity of all existence.

Thus, the device is ready to use, guiding you to reconnect with the eternal truth of "Aham asmi" — I exist, and in this existence, I am whole.

Amma Says *"However, unlike the worm, humans exploit and destroy nature. we should enquire into the very source of the power that makes even the intellect function. That power exists within. It is the very substratum of our existence - and our existence cannot be denied. The existence of the world, the existence of everything in nature, cannot be denied. The truth "I exist" is self-evident. You may deny God*

by saying, "God is just a belief," But existence cannot be refuted. That existence, that Cosmic Power , is God."
27th Convocation Day - Amritapuri Campus - August 31, 2024

Conclusion

Can such a device exist? As we use the Upanishads as our reference, are there references in the Upanishads that would negate this possibility? The Upanishads emphasize the need for direct realization and inner experience, suggesting that our True Nature is beyond any physical device. Yet, as a metaphorical representation, this device can serve as a powerful reminder and guiding tool to help individuals reconnect with their true self, reflecting the timeless essence of the Upanishads in a way that resonates with modern life.

"I exist" stands as a beacon of truth in the ever-changing landscape of human experience. It is a reminder of our inherent divinity, our eternal connection to the cosmic whole. In recognizing this truth, we awaken to the boundless potential of our own consciousness and realize that, in the end, "I exist" is not just a statement of fact but a profound revelation of the timeless essence of being.

"This device is the gentle grace of existence, we are but threads woven into the matrix of time, connecting past, present, and future generations. Each moment is adorned with the blessings of our ancestors, their whispered wisdom echoing through the ages. As we stand in the embrace of this sacred lineage, gratitude becomes the melody of our souls, a testament to our presence here and now. And in the symphony of eternity, our reverence for those who came before us becomes the legacy we give to the generations yet to unfold, a timeless beacon of love, light, and remembrance."

Thus, the device is ready to use, guiding you to reconnect with the eternal truth of "Aham asmi" — I exist, and in this existence, I am whole. This device, inspired by the teachings of the Upanishads, serves as a bridge between ancient wisdom and modern life, reminding us of our unchanging, eternal essence amidst the transient nature of existence.

Disclaimer: This is not a tool to help us determine the morality of any given situation. Morality is established by the constitution, justice system, and legal frameworks that set the rules for citizens to follow. Reward and punishment depend on the verdict given according to the law of the country, so unless proven guilty, no one can be named as an offender. Therefore, it is not about Punya and Papam (merit and sin) as described in ancient scriptures; rather, it is the freedom of the country that sets the rules to follow, not age-old scriptures.

On Morality

Morality, in its essence, is a complex and evolving concept shaped by the collective conscience of society and enshrined in the legal frameworks of a nation. It transcends the ancient dichotomy of merit and sin, Punya and Papam, embracing a more dynamic understanding rooted in the principles of justice, equality, and freedom. The constitution and legal systems are the pillars upon which modern morality stands, ensuring that every individual is judged fairly and impartially.

In the modern world, morality is not a static set of commandments but a living dialogue between the governed and their governors, constantly refined by the values of liberty, dignity, and human rights. The laws of a country are crafted to reflect the ethical standards of its time, protecting individuals and fostering a just society. This framework allows for the fair administration of justice, where rewards and punishments are meted out based on evidence and the rule of law, rather than ancient edicts.

Thus, while spiritual and religious texts provide historical perspectives on right and wrong, it is the legal structures of a nation that ultimately govern moral conduct in society today.

By ensuring that laws are just, transparent, and inclusive, we uphold a moral order that respects the freedom and dignity of every individual. This approach to morality, grounded in legal principles, safeguards our rights and responsibilities, fostering a society where justice prevails over prejudice and fairness over tradition.

Swami Amritachitswarupananda Puri

www.ingramcontent.com/pod-product-compliance
Lightning Source LLC
LaVergne TN
LVHW051551080426
835510LV00020B/2947